20 AMAZING PLANTS

AND THEIR PRACTICAL USES

RACHEL CORBY

20 AMAZING PLANTS
AND THEIR PRACTICAL USES

Published by The Good Life Press Ltd. 2011

Text copyright © Rachel Corby
Photographs (unless otherwise credited) copyright © Stephen Studd
www.stephenstuddphotography.com

ISBN 978 1 90487 1940

A catalogue record for this book is available from
the British Library.

Published by
The Good Life Press Ltd.
The Old Pigsties
Clifton Fields
Lytham Road
Preston
PR4 0XG

www.goodlifepress.co.uk
www.homefarmer.co.uk

Front cover (top row) Middle shot - Hazel Chair made by Dave Jackson
2nd row, (left to right) Woven lime bast by Richard de Trey-White,
Hazel Pencils made by Dave Jackson, Walnut carving by Guido Oakley
Bottom row (left to right) Hazel dibber made by Dave Jackson, Willow sculpture by Tom Hare
Chestnut chair made by Richard de Trey-White

Back cover (left to right) Willow baskets made by Norah Kennedy,
Monkey puzzle lamp made by John Bennison, Lime bast stool made by Richard de Trey-White

CONTENTS

Acknowledgments

Resources

Glossary

ACKNOWLEDGEMENTS

Firstly I would like to thank my friends Jay and Simon for voicing their disapointment that hemp did not appear in my first book (The Medicine Garden) as their comments provided the seed that grew into this book. Thanks to Patrick Whitefield for his advice and encouragement. Many thanks once again to Stephen Studd for the time and energy spent on the beautiful photography and the suggestion that I include walnut.

There are certain crafts people I would like to thank for being so generous with their time and knowledge and also allowing us to photograph their work. Richard de Trey-White for the sweet chestnut chair and woven lime bast, Guido Oakley for his beautiful walnut sculpture, Tom Hare for his amazing willow structure and John Bennison for his amazing monkey puzzle lamp. Special thanks to Dave Jackson for all his time and the hazel coppice crafts. Also to Norah Kennedy for letting us photograph some of her baskets and visit a couple of her workshops. Finally, many thanks to Frans Brown for his incredible enthusiasm and supplying us with photogaphs of his hand turned monkey puzzle bowls.

This book is dedicated to everyone who believes in a better future and is prepared to put in the work to get there.

DISCLAIMER

This book is sold for information purposes only; it is not intended to diagnose any condition. It is essential to always get a professional diagnosis for any ongoing symptoms. If you are currently on medication, always check with a naturally oriented healthcare professional before using plant medicines. They will be able to advise you on any possible interactions between prescribed medicines and plant medicines and any potential side effects of taking them alongside each other. Read the notes in italics at the bottom of each medicine section before choosing to use the remedies described and exercise special caution if you are pregnant or breast feeding. If you start to have any adverse reactions to a plant medicine you are using, cease use immediately and seek professional advice.

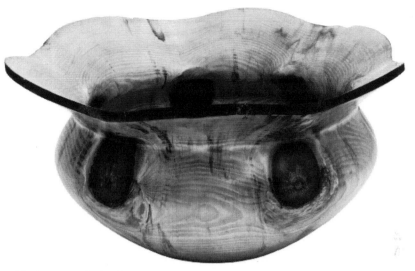

Monkey puzzle bowl, made and photographed by Frans Brown.

INTRODUCTION

I AM FASCINATED by the plant world; to me all plants are amazing. I have spent many years learning of the food and medicine plants offer and during this process a whole host of other uses for plants have crept into my consciousness. They surround us, providing us with oxygen to breathe and food to eat (even the most ardent meat eater would go hungry if there were no plants to feed the animals!). It has perhaps been forgotten or overlooked in recent times that plants can provide a whole lot more. At one time the majority of our housing, tools, utensils, clothing, medicines, and even soaps and resins were made from plant based materials. During the twentieth century chemical and synthetic products began to gain prominence. Oil based products were developed and became easier and cheaper to mass produce than plant based alternatives, replacing them for the most part. But the age of cheap oil is coming to an end. Plants have always been and always will be renewable due to their nature. They constantly grow, with new growth replacing harvested sections or entire new plants coming into being from simply sowing their seed. The materials harvested from each plant can be viewed as resources, and definitively renewable resoures. This book takes you on a journey which looks at just 20 plants, at the materials they provide and the plethora of practical uses they can be put to.

As this planet rumbles at an ever accelerating rate to a future where we will undoubtedly experience an increasing scarcity of resources it makes sense to look at what things are made from, how they are made and what alternatives are available. My aim is to raise awareness of how we can look after ourselves a little better by becoming a little more self reliant, stepping away from the insecurity of a society which is seemingly dependent upon the use of non renewable resources. Oil is ancient sunlight, a valuable and finite resource and yet materials made from it currently form the majority of the objects we use on a daily basis. Not only that but items produced far from home are transported to the retail outlets, from which we purchase them, with fuel made from the same diminishing oil reserves. Our consumer choices play a part in the world's skirmishes and squabbles for rights over the last few profitable stocks of oil. Our choices as consumers are valuable, they do matter. Plants as mentioned are, by their fast growing nature, a renewable resource. Items made from plants still form a much greater proportion of the objects used on a daily basis in some cultures. The more we grow and process

closer to home, the more we return to an understanding of the intrinsic, the true value of the objects we use in our daily lives and often take for granted. The process of working with natural materials, from watching seeds germinate to creating a finished product, can be enjoyable and incredibly rewarding. Through a raised sense of awareness of each stage, each process, my hope is that a greater sense of respect for and balance with the rest of the natural world can be achieved. It is interesting to note that all plant made items will, with time, biodegrade naturally, but unlike chemical and oil based products, will not cause pollution or further degradation of the environment in so doing – instead they will just decompose, becoming soil and feeding a new cycle. To see and respect plants as renewable resources, tapping into their potential and finding practical uses for them is part of a sustainable, and a better future for us all.

I have witnessed huge scars on tropical hillsides where the excavation of roads has caused erosion, the orange earth from a distance looking more like blood, slowly, silently dripping from an open wound. I have planted vetiver grass, with its vast and strong root network, along the contours of such degraded hillsides to hold the earth in place. I subsequently discovered that this grass is not just great for erosion control, but also provides weed supression, beneficial symbiotic relationships with other plants, mulch, thatch, essential oil, medicine, fodder, fuel and the raw material for weaving all kinds of handicrafts. What an incredible plant and yet it is not alone.

Willow Sculpture by Tom Hare.

"We are literally surrounded by plants that have a multitude of uses, that are indeed brimming with a wealth of renewable resources".

Certain plants stand out from others due to their individual characteristics which make them more useful to us. The coconut palm, for example, is known in Malaysia as *pokok seribu guna*, which translates as tree of a thousand uses. The tropics, where the coconut palm grows, is very rich in plant life with a huge diversity of species, however plants with a wide range of uses are not just limited to that climatic zone. In the deserts of the South West USA, which to the untrained eye are just full of dried out old scrub and cacti, there are a plethora of incredible plants with multiple uses. The Agave, for example, provides a range of foods, fibre for making rope, baskets and mats, even the distilled juice of the young flower stalks is utilised, constituting the main ingredient in Tequila. There is a large amount of information available regarding plants in tropical and subtropical regions, but as a keen gardener in the process of downscaling to a more simple life I have found a sizable gap in information on the uses of temperate climate plants. This book has been written for the earth's temperate regions in response to that information gap.

7

The temperate zone is widely defined as the area between the Tropic of Cancer and the Arctic Circle in the northern hemisphere and the Tropic of Capricorn and the Antarctic Circle in the southern hemisphere. In addition to the geographical location, classification as temperate requires that for a minimum of four months of the year the temperature is consistently above 10°C (50°F). This clearly covers a huge area with widely differing local conditions, which are complicated and subdivided by the effects of latitude, altitude and aspect. Suffice to say that the temperate zone houses a large proportion of the world's population and in reality a huge range of different climates. If you take two separate areas with only 10 or 20 miles between them you will find microclimates that will support some plant species in one but not the other. In fact even within your own garden you will find temperature differentiations caused by frost pockets or sun traps, so you will need to remain observant and open to experimentation to find the optimum position for any plant you grow. In this book I have focused on plants that will grow within the UK, either happily and naturally or with a little gentle persuasion such as a greenhouse or winter protection. Other areas within the temperate zone can have a much greater or narrower temperature range

INTRODUCTION

and so you may need to adjust the type and degree of care for the plants I have detailed to thriv

The bulk of this book is a plant directory which provides an in depth look at just 20 plants. It illustrates the abundance of resources a single plant can contain and how by choosing a select few of these incredible plants you can provide for a large proportion of your needs, naturally and in a relatively small space. Plant based materials can be used not only to feed, clothe and medicate ourselves but also to build our homes, furnish and heat them. It has been a difficult process choosing which plants to focus on as I wanted to represent each of these categories but am also acutely aware that each plant is unique and provides multiple resources not just to humans but to other animal, bird, insect and of course plant life. In the end the plants I have chosen are ones that I deem to have especially great riches or unique characteristics.

Many of the uses listed such as dye, paper making or yarn may seem a somewhat whimsical reference to a bygone age where we had to create everything from that which was growing around us. The fact that the plants listed have these properties may seem irrelevant or just a curiosity for people experimenting in the crafts. But who is to say what we will

need to provide for ourselves in the future, in perhaps 10 or 20 years time when the seeds you plant and nuture now stand tall as a grove of mature trees? Even if you just hold this knowledge as a potential in the back of your mind, planting your land with these or other similarly useful species may smooth your existence in later life or benefit future generations who could face shortages of resources that we cannot even imagine. The truth is we can still buy anything and everything we need and want in a baffling array of sizes, colours and styles for very little financial output, but at what cost?

Through researching this book I have come to a new understanding of the value of many everyday items. It is amazing that we have reached a place of such abundance in the west that, for example, we all have multiple outfits for every occasion. Growing fibre crops oneself and realising what goes into the creation of each garment is quite revolutionary. During the last century machinery has made processing ever cheaper and taken each of us away from the source, away from knowing what really goes into what we are wearing (and throwing away). When it comes to fabrics it may be interesting to note that cotton currently accounts for 90% of the fibre that is produced every year, however despite

Chestnut chair made by Richard de Trey-White.

The chapter on flax details extracting the fibres, spinning them into yarn and then weaving fabric, a hugely long and time consuming process. Yet I think learning about what goes into the production of fabric from the moment the seed is planted all the way through to wearing the finished garment adds such a deep level of respect and value and an understanding of all the time and energy that goes into its creation. Getting in touch with what it takes to produce just one item of clothing may make you change the way you view and value your wardrobe and will perhaps change your spending habits on clothing for good. It has certainly made me stop and think. Perhaps part of the answer to the global ecological crisis is that we all need to get back in touch with where things come from and treat every piece of fabric with the respect that something involving so much work deserves. This enhanced sence of value may help change our perception, so that we demand and use less and at the end of the garment's life, when it's not even fit for the charity shop, find a way of reusing our rags. They can be used as tea towels, cleaning cloths, made into rag rugs and if they are made from natural fibres they can be incorporated into the garden as a slow rotting mulch.

being a natural fibre it has a huge environmental impact. It is very water hungry and requires a hot climate. Much of the world's supply comes from India, Pakistan, China and Sudan where water is often scarce. To irrigate the cotton valuable water supplies are often diverted from elsewhere causing drought conditions and salinisation. In addition conventionally grown cotton is responsible for 20% of the world's pesticide use, not forgetting the petrochemical based fertilisers necessary to make it a commercially viable crop. One alternative is to grow fibre crops closer to home, ones that don't require as much water or even a fraction of the polluting chemicals, and equally importantly do not need transporting half way around the planet.

Of course it is not just fabric

but so many other everyday items that can be made from plants. Cosmetics are a good example as petrochemicals and known carcinogens have crept into the majority of hair and skin care products.

"It can be incredibly empowering to realise we can grow materials and use them to provide for many of our needs, as our forefathers once did".

Making your own from natural ingredients will ensure that the products you use on your body and that are subsequently absorbed through your skin really are protecting and enhancing your natural beauty rather than causing yet another toxic hazard for the environment and your internal system to clean up. I encourage each reader to look at what you need and use on a daily basis and have a go at making some of those things from plant materials grown by yourselves. Being involved

in the process from seed to finished product you develop a new or enhanced sense, not only of value but also of connection, which in turn leads to a greater reverence for the raw materials, the plants themselves.

This book has been written for those people who find themselves, like me, yearning for a simpler, nature based life – the good life! To move away from MDF, plastics and other factory made oil and chemical based products that pollute our world with a noxious chemical cocktail and instead fill our homes, wardrobes, dinner tables and medicine chests with beautiful products lovingly handcrafted from natural materials.

The research and writing of this book has been an incredible and inspirational journey. I have met a vast array of skilled crafts people from paper makers to sculptors and woodsmen. I have learned so much and realised that there is a huge craft network that is alive, evolving and thriving. These people are experts in their field and it is easy to see they have a genuine love of their craft and the materials they use. Many of them share their skills through workshops which in itself is a valuable resource for us all (see resources).

This book is intended to provide advice and accessible

information for anyone tending a patch of land from a tiny backyard or an allotment, to several acres. Even if all you have available is a shelf in the kitchen I have included some plants whose seed can be sprouted into nutritious food with no outside space necessary. If this is your situation then why not join the growing movement of guerilla gardeners and plant some useful species in public places. They may or may not survive, but if they do imagine harvesting your first nuts from a tree you planted in the park! Equally some plants such as stinging nettle can be foraged from wild or derelict spaces and others such as willow can be purchased as withies ready for craft use directly from suppliers.

The directory is not a definitive list of 20 plants that everyone should have but rather a collection of suggestions to encourage you to think outside the box when planning your planting. Choose to furnish your outside space with plants viewed more broadly than simply on the basis of their edible or aesthetic value. Grow plants that can fulfill more than one of your needs and use your available space wisely. Become more aware of the possibilities and renewable resources that you can grow, harvest and process in your own backyard.

WHY WE NEED RENEWABLE RESOURCES, AND WHY NOW

SOCIETY IS SO developed and in many senses advanced due in part to the fact that we are so proficient at finding, mining and utilising minerals, metals, coal and oil from deep within the Earth. Unfortunately the availability of such resources is finite and often their extraction and processing can be devastating for the local ecology and heavily polluting on a wider scale. Rare earth metals such as promethium, neodymium and many more are built into magnets, motors and batteries which are at the core of nearly all our electronic gadgetry, including renewable energy devices such as solar panels and wind turbines. Even energy saving light bulbs contain terbium. The mining of these metals can be so polluting that it undermines the green credentials of the finished products, creating a dilemma, to say the least.

Oil is probably the non renewable resource that as a society we are currently most dependent upon, without until recently perhaps even noticing or acknowledging its finite supply. But we are fast approaching or have even surpassed the point of peak oil, the point where supply begins to be limited by the physical restraints on conventional oil production. When it comes to oil we all contribute: we all use oil based products, drive in oil fueled cars and eat food that has been transported to market with that same fuel. As the demand for oil continues to grow and stocks dwindle, ever more expensive and environmentally damaging extraction methods will be used, exploiting tar sands for example. The immediate consequence for consumers will be a rise in prices. Plastics, glues, resins and chemicals are all, for the most part, made from hydrocarbon fuels. Even products made from wood are likely to have been painted, preserved or dyed with chemicals made from natural gas or petroleum. The more energy reliant and material based your lifestyle is, the more wallet shock you will experience. So to avoid an energy crisis as oil becomes harder to extract and prices increase, changes need to be made to our homes and how we live.

The consequences of our over reliance on petroleum and its derivatives go beyond personal finances, encompassing air, soil and water pollution as well as knock on impacts on human health. Common chemicals in plastics, for example, are disrupting the hormonal balance, causing a huge rise in reproductive defects not just in other species but also in ourselves and our children.

Disposable household products are for the most part made from oil based plastics. How are they disposable? They do not biodegrade for hundreds or thousands of years and they are made from a precious and diminishing resource. How is it that they can possibly be marketed as disposable and we believe the hype? How diminished has our sense of value become that we think something so precious can be used once and then thrown away? Food is another issue: the majority is grown using vast quantities of petrochemicals. In many instances it is grown far from market, requiring yet more oil based resources to reach our tables. These facts put us in a vulnerable position, enhanced by the dissociation many people have with how and where their food was grown.

We are living in a time of growing alienation from the rest of the natural world. We are experiencing the fastest and one of the largest scale mass extinctions the planet has ever known combined with habitat loss, pollution and accelerated climate change. These challenges have at least in part been caused by the actions of humankind and are occuring alongside a global depletion of finite (or non renewable) resources. This has created a new kind of crisis, different from any we have faced as a species as this time it's truly global, encompassing the entire planet. It is becoming clear that our current behaviour and consumption patterns are unsustainable, even in the short term. Yet when you look around and see all the waste of energy and resouces that characterize Western society, it can seem overwhelming, or even that there is no point in trying to make changes.

There are a vast number of initiatives, online social networking groups and non governmental organisations that are focusing on environmental issues and taking action. Environmental scientists have developed techniques and methods designed to repair and regenerate degraded ecosystems. More and more items are being recycled and non polluting renewable energy sources are being tapped. These admirable developments are far reaching and yet, without a change in our collective philosophical approach, indeed the entire paradigm within which we conduct our lives, the efforts mentioned will never be enough. A revolution of consciousness is required so that the current world order can be superseded by a truely compassionate global culture. The emphasis needs to shift from one where humanity seeks domination over natural systems to one where we protect, encourage and work with them, respecting their

integrity and understanding their intrinsic value and the fact that we are a living, breathing part of them. In a sense it is about recognising the sacredness and interconnectedness of all life and acting accordingly.

So what can we as individual citizens of Planet Earth do when the world's governments cannot even come to agreements over actions, instead spending their time arguing out the facts and apportioning blame? Well I for one believe that change must start with ourselves. As Lao-tzu once said: "A journey of a thousand miles begins with a single step". The most effective way we can contribute is for each of us to take responsibility for ourselves and the daily impact we have on this planet and make the changes we need globally in our own lives. Taking responsibility is key as when it's in the hands of others it becomes easy to moan at the outcome and apportion blame. In handing over responsibility we have given something vital away and it is common to feel unable to act. Over time our ambition, motivation, even dreams seem to drain away. Somehow we have given responsibility to the great machine – the multinationals, the governments, the financial institutions – and have become powerless to act against it. Our little voices never seem to be heard. But it is our world. We are made from it, our skin is made from the flesh of the earth, from the stones, soil, sunlight, water, plants, insects and animals. We are made from all the life we share this planet with, that we exchange cells with, that we eat, drink and breathe. With so much going on it is important to remember that we are an intrinsic, integral part of this world, not separate from it or immune from what we subject it to. No matter what the machine may try to convince you they cannot, indeed no one can, be arrogant enough to assume they understand the intricacies of the vast, interdependent network of life that is this planet. One cannot discount a single life form, individual or species and say that it's expendable, that it's not important in the grand scheme of things, that we can let that one go. Ever played Jenga? How many bricks can you pull from the stack before the whole lot topples into total disarray? Life has been described as a web connecting all the different elements and species. How many threads dare we let the machine cut before we are left as a species dangling in peril and all alone? The Hopi saying "We are the ones we've been waiting for" comes to mind.

The first step to reclaiming our power and individual sense of responsibility is education. The first plastics came from plants and cellophane actually got its name from cellulose found in plant cell walls. It was only in the 1920s that the majority of biochemicals used in industry were replaced with petrochemicals. Substituting our use of petrochemicals back to biochemicals is possible but it must evolve alongside a sustainable ethos and a shift in consumer demand to really become a viable, non polluting alternative. Enough agricultural wastes are currently created to feed the industry with raw materials, enough to break the hold of petrochemicals and almost entirely replace them. That is without cultivating a single extra field, just being more careful with what is discarded and finding appropriate uses for that which agriculture and industry currently regard as waste.

Individually as consumers there is much we can do. Start seeking out plant based plastics and change spending patterns so that the products purchased are of good quality and have the potential to last a lifetime. Small changes in the perception of our material needs, the products we use and the materials they are made from can make all the difference. Wood when well crafted will last for generations, and although fashions and styles may change, bespoke items of furniture can be handed down as heirlooms (as happened in

WHY WE NEED RENEWABLE RESOURCES

the past), surely a superior choice than buying creations from MDF or plastic that break more easily and end up in landfill.

"I have taken much inspiration from other cultures where money and material wealth is scarce, out of necessity nothing is wasted and there is a use for everything".

Traditional nomadic Mongolians do not even spill a drop of blood when slaughtering their animals because everything is precious. Many cultures are fantastic at finding new uses for things that in the West are often discarded, making sandals from old tyres for example. It is possible to learn from these societies, to become more creative and frugal with what we have and to tap the potential renewable resources that plants around us provide.

16

To further reduce our dependence on oil most homes will need improvements in energy efficiency. One way is to insulate well and this can be done with the material provided from some of the plants in the directory, spelt and hemp especially jump to mind. Even reused and reprocessed old plastic drinks bottles are now commercially available as an insulation material and that is clearly a better place for them than in landfill. New homes need to be designed with passive solar heating in mind and again can be built from and insulated by some of the plants in the directory. We can use the sun to heat our water, certainly in the summer months. Finding large scale solutions is beyond the scope of this book and it seems beyond the grasp of those currently in power. But there is a need for a new paradigm, for taking matters into our own hands and building the small scale changes into our homes and our lives and doing it now.

Perhaps as oil prices increase we will all have no option but to source our food more locally. Maybe conventional agriculture will switch back to organic methods as the price of petrochemicals make its produce less competitive than produce grown without them. Whichever way growing some of your own food will help you to become more self reliant and less dependant on the

Walnut carving by Guido Oakley.

20 AMAZING PLANTS

volatile and changing world market. Of course it would be difficult to be completely self-sufficient in food without addressing our concept of needs as opposed to wants, especially as we have become acustomed to exotic fruits, vegetables and grains that would be difficult to produce ourselves. However it is easy to grow at least some of what you eat. Even if you only have a few pots available as a growing space you may be surprised at what you can produce and how rewarding it is to take back at least some control over what reaches your table.

As a society in general our skills, knowledge and ability to meet our basic needs has atrophied. Our skills and knowledge are adapted to suit our modern lives and have become more computer orientated which does have the benefit of the vast resources of information available at our fingertips on the Internet. Yet as we become more distant from the source, from direct interaction with plant harvests, how things are made, repaired and reused, we become more vulnerable and in a sense more useless. We can go out and earn money (depending on the job market) but can't provide for our needs at home. As financial markets are unstable and in crisis, hyper inflation may become a possibility.

To be more secure a greater level of practical skills and knowledge will become more useful and perhaps one day will be more valuable than money! For me this is more than just a back up plan but a movement towards a more self reliant future. There is a diversity of options with which to tackle the scarcity of resources and environmental problems we currently face, and are even more likely to face in the future. Learning skills and providing for ourselves with renewable plant resources is at least in part one. Realistically our whole philosophical approach has to change. As individual citizens every purchase we make is a vote, as it appears money speaks most loudly to those in power. Planting our gardens, allotments, smallholdings and parks with resource rich plants, learning to utilize those resources and understanding the true value of them is a positive way to say no to the skirmish for the last drops of oil and will offer us a more stable future.

The world we know is at crisis point and yet it is still easy to blame and feel powerless or to ignore or even deny what's happening. But if each of us does not individually choose to stand up and opt for a different future, then who will? Choosing to use plants and their products is the sustainable, renewable option and will preserve the supply of finite resources a little longer, allowing our lifestyles time to adapt and alternative Earth friendly technologies to be developed. Plants interact healthily as part of the ecosystem and they can be harvested and replaced without the side effects that occur when plundering the Earth's non renewable resources. Respectfully growing and using plants to provide for our needs is building a future based on renewable resources instead of the ever dwindling stocks of ancient sunlight. A feeling of connection to the rest of nature occurs naturally when working with plants and it becomes more difficult to act disrespectfully, to pillage resources and pollute our environment and our bodies. A natural shift occurs to one of more harmonious coexistence. This is the philosophical change I am talking of. Adopted on a wide scale this would make a significant difference to humanitiy's current predicament. Yet the only place each of us can start is with ourselves and our immediate environment. Don't become overwhelmed trying to save the world. Taking responsibility for yourself and your actions can make all the difference, and will set the wheels in motion for the change that needs to occur on a planetary scale.

WORKING WITH PLANTS AND THEIR INHERENT RESOURCES

ONE OF THE first and most important points to note when working with plants is that they are not just here to be used by us and not to be considered solely as resources for our own use. The plants listed in the directory are just suggestions and it is not intended that you fill your immediate environment with these plants alone. You will need other plants to give you a wide and varied diet but so too do all the other animals and insects that have a part to play in a healthy ecosystem.

I have been incredibly inspired by the permaculture movement and tend to cultivate my outside space from this perspective and encourage you to do the same. In brief the idea is to design your planting with respect for nature, working with natural systems rather than against them. It basically involves mimicking patterns and associations that are found in nature which in turn leads to a stronger and more resilient overall system. It is also about utilising all the space available, both vertical and horizontal, whilst finding plants that will grow in the shade of taller ones or create other beneficial conditions in which different species can thrive. Growing organically

20 AMAZING PLANTS

is also an intrinsic part of permaculture and incredibly important, especially if you are planning on consuming your plants as food or medicine. Using chemicals during your growing will have an impact on the environment and in turn your personal health but will also affect the integrity of the plant. Plants that are allowed to grow without the use of petrochemical based herbicides, pesticides and fertilisers will be stronger as they will have had to rely on their inherent strength for their survival (with perhaps just a little nurturing from you in the form of watering and weeding!). To make it easier plan growing plants that attract pollinators, repel pests and parts of which can be used to make organic feed, weed suppressing and water conserving mulch or be composted to produce lovely, rich soil for your next set of seedlings. Using plants in this way will help your outside space to become more self sustaining. For me this philosophy also encompasses finding a multitude of uses for everything that I choose to plant or otherwise find growing. A diverse output, whether for yourself or intended for market, makes you much less vulnerable to change or crop failure.

Anyone who has ever grown a food crop such as a cucumber, which takes only a couple of months to produce fruit from the day the seed is sown, will have experienced an enhanced level of pleasure and respect for the simple fruit. You find yourself rejoicing at its germination and cherishing the day of harvest, then savouring the delicate and subtle fragrance whilst relishing the refreshing flavours, alongside its crunchy texture and cooling sensations. You will know what I am expressing if you have felt this joy. So imagine planting a seed and waiting years, 5, 10 or 40 even, before harvesting your first crop of nuts – imagine the level of love and respect you will have built by then. Suddenly the value of a simple nut skyrockets within you as over the years you begin to understand what it takes – how many rotations of the earth around its axis, around the sun and how much rainfall and sunshine. Your first bite will be more than a little taste of heaven, more a grasp of the universe in all its complexity. When you grow a plant from seed, nurture it during its early days and care for it throughout its growth, you are constantly building your relationship with that plant and the material you will eventually harvest from it. Even if you are wild harvesting the care you give and the enjoyment you receive become an exchange which adds a degree of 'livingness' to the whole process. It makes you feel more alive and deepens your interactions with the world you inhabit.

Get to know each plant because they are more than just a storehouse of resources; they are living beings. Take one plant at a time and start to build your relationship. Observe it through the seasons, watch it change and grow and start to listen. You will hear when it needs water, shade and even a section pruned or removed; it will call you and tell you if you are listening. Most often you will experience it as a conscious thought as you pass by the plant, but it is more than plain observation and logic; it is a feeling, a communication. In time you will hear that communication even when you are not in close proximity to the plant. You may be away visiting friends for the weekend and suddenly a strong thought of plant a, b or c will arise and you will know that it is in need of something. On your return you will rush to that plant and most likely find yourself talking to it as you water it or collect fallen fruit, performing the task you were prompted to do. Relating to plants in this way truly enriches your life.

It is not only during the growing of the plants but also during the processing, the making of something with the plant material, be it a chair or a loaf of bread, that I encourage you to be conscious and present. As you hold your harvest in your hand, get to know the materials. Touch

them, feel them and smell them. Close your eyes and explore them with your hands, feel the material, experience its texture, its strength, its character. In this way you will get to know and understand the material and you will be inspired as to new possibilities of how you can work with it and what you can create. When working in this way with the material it takes on a life and an energy and becomes a living being that you can work with, touching, feeling and sensing it at all times. As you give yourself to this process and the material yields under your direction, something invisible is exchanged between you. Somehow you become very much a part of that chair, that bread, and it too becomes very much a part of you. Whatever it is you are making will absorb some of your (the maker's) energy. As a result your relationship with the raw material, the living plant, deepens irrevocably. Your soul is enriched and the separation cast by the current cultural paradigm between yourself and the rest of the natural world narrows slightly. It can be your little secret, your special relationship as you pass the chair you made and lovingly brush your hands across it, or say a prayer of gratitude as you eat your freshly baked bread. The next time you are in the presence of the material's origin, the plant itself, a smile will touch the corners of your lips as you silently yet wholeheartedly greet that old friend, admire its beauty and fuss lovingly around it as the bond grows ever stronger. Whatever you produce will be more sympathetic to the nature of the material and ultimately more beautiful as a result.

"Working with plants and their harvest does not just fulfill our material but also our spiritual needs".

I have not listed the beneficial effects of working with plants on mental health in the medicine sections for each plant but they are well known. Gardening has become a recognised therapy for depression, recovering drug addicts and young people with behavioral disorders. A friend of mine was once asked by her therapist whether she had any plants in the bedroom. When she replied yes the therapist suggested that was perhaps the reason why she was having difficulty finding a member of the opposite sex as a companion, because she already had companionship in the bedroom! Although

Hazel chair made by Dave Jackson

20 AMAZING PLANTS

I make light of it, it is true that you do feel the calming presence of plants if you share a room with them. They help to boost your mental health, your sense of connection and place in the world and they calm you in your most distraught moments. There are few people who will not find a walk in the woods or the wild intensely calming and reassuring if they are stressed or experiencing a challenging emotional state. I would consider interaction with plants an essential part of our well being. The further apart our individual connection has drifted, the less we know about where our food, clothing, furniture etc. come from and what ithey are made from and the more societal ills, violent crime, substance abuse and mental health issues arise. Perhaps I am reading too much into it but the truth remains that the less connection we have with the natural world, the more challenges society seems to face. I defy anyone who grows plants and makes things from them to not feel good, to not find some kind of therapeutic benefit whether they are looking for it or not. Throughout the whole process of working with plants the moments of nurture and crafting become not chores, or hobbies even, but works of art, moments of bliss where your whole self is absorbed and immersed in the magical process of sharing and creating.

The uses in the lists for each plant are suggestions, ideas and examples of what I or others have done. Try them, experiment and then find your own. Try with the plants in the directory and others, as perhaps you don't have the climate, space or patience to grow each one. As your relationship with the plants you are growing and using develops it will become natural to ask and thank when harvesting. It is sometimes necessary to take the life of a plant to utilise one of its resources and then, more than ever, I recommend thanking wholeheartedly for the ultimate gift, the life of the plant itself to fulfill one of your needs. As you allow the plants and their materials to get under your skin, every day becomes a living prayer as your life is filled with their produce and all you have made with it. You will begin to think of the plants on a daily basis throughout the seasons, even if you do not venture outside but are just thankfully using the items you have created from their resources. As your relationship with both the plant and the materials deepens you will find yourself spending the long dark winter months dreaming up improvements and different uses to try with the following year's harvest.

24

ALFALFA
(Medicago sativa)

THE NAME OF this plant comes from the arabic *alf-al-fa* which translates as *father of all foods*. The arabs at one time considered it a sacred plant and fed it to their horses in the belief that it would impart stamina, swiftness and wisdom. In folklore alfalfa is a bringer of prosperity and keeping some dried leaves in your home is said to protect the dwellers from hunger, poverty and unhappiness.

Alfalfa seeds are in fact tiny beans, the smallest member of the legume family. It is the most cultivated legume in the world, appearing everywhere from sprouting trays in middle class urban kitchens to the banks of high altitude desert streams.

VARIETIES

Medicago sativa
Common names include Spanish clover, California clover and Lucerne.

There are many modern cultivars and the following are all very winter hardy:

Iroquois – resistant to bacterial wilt

Kansas – drought resistant

Ranger – resistant to bacterial wilt

Vernal – resistant to bacterial wilt with high yields

Growth Habits

Alfalfa is a drought resistant perennial legume with a lifespan of 3-20 years (depending on variety). It grows to a height of around 1m and prefers a position in full sun. It will not thrive in acidic or waterlogged soils but will grow in most other soils, even those that are nutritionally depleted. The optimum conditions for growth are a well drained, sandy loam soil with a pH of around 7. Growth is restricted by particularly heavy soils or the presence of a shallow hardpan.

Sow any time from early spring to mid summer at a rate of 3g per m². The grown plant has a resemblance to clover, albeit much taller. It has small clusters of purple flowers which appear in June or July. Alfalfa is auto-toxic, which means that it becomes difficult to replant with its own kind, so you will need to give each area that has grown alfalfa a rest before trying to grow it there again.

Maintenance

Being relatively disease resistant and out competing most weeds, alfalfa needs very little maintenance, only a little weeding in the early stages.

Harvesting, Processing and Storage

Seeds are ready to harvest from July until September. Collect them when the seed pods look dry and are starting to open.

Harvest greens as needed throughout the growing season. If you are intending to dry some of the leaf for later use, harvest before flowering and dry in bunches out of direct sunlight. Both dried leaves and seed should be stored in airtight containers in a cool dark place.

Uses

Food

Alfalfa is one of the easiest seeds (or beans!) to sprout. Simply soak them overnight then drain and place in a sprouter or a fine weave bamboo basket. If you don't have either then a pint glass will do. Rinse and drain thoroughly every day and more regularly if it is really hot. After a day or two you will see fine white tails emerging from the seed. These are the sprouts. Wait for 5-7 days until the sprouts have a pair of dark green leaves. At this point they are ready to eat. Add them to salads, sandwiches and as a topping on soups. They can be added to super healthy green smoothies; just blend with the rest of the ingredients.

If you sprouted too many to use all at once they may be refrigerated for a few days or juiced along with other fruits or vegetables in a good quality juicer. I have even dehydrated them (this must be done at a temperature of 40°C (105°F) or below to preserve the healthy enzymes) and then ground them to a powder so that I can shake a little over my food, adding an enzyme rich treat to my meals when on the move. Being sprouts they are a living food and so retain many more nutrients than a vegetable that has been harvested days or weeks in advance. Alfalfa is high in chlorophyll and has a high vitamin A, B-complex, C, E, K, calcium, iron, magnesium, potassium and phosphorus content and so is an extremely healthy addition to the diet. The unsprouted seed can be ground and added to flour mixes to improve the protein content.

The greenery can be juiced for a full power chlorophyll rich blast. Combine it with other vegetable juices to suit your taste. The young leaves and shoots can be added raw to salads or steamed and eaten as a vegetable.

MEDICINE

Juice a of handful of sprouts 3 times a day, mixing with other juice, and drink as a tonic to build strength when convalescing. Adding alfalfa sprouts regularly to the diet can help reduce cholesterol levels (specifically LDLs) and blood pressure.

Juice the leaves to help improve circulatory, respiratory and sinus problems. Drinking an infusion made from the leaves can help improve the symptoms of gout, rheumatism and some forms of arthritis, whilst lowering blood sugar levels, helping to heal ulcers and stimulating lactation in breast feeding mothers. It helps balance the hormones and so is a beneficial tea to drink during menopause and if suffering from PMS. It helps calcium retention in the bones so can be used to help guard against the development of osteoporosis. It helps relax the nerves, making it a soothing bedtime brew. It cleanses the blood, improving the condition of anyone suffering from fatigue and in addition it is soothing to the digestion and will help reduce water retention.

Do not drink alfalfa continuously over long periods of time and avoid it if you have an auto-immune disease, lupus, rheumatoid arthritis or are pregnant.

FUEL

Alfalfa has the potential to be fermented and made into cellulosic ethanol (see p172) which can then be used as a

27

fuel to replace or supplement petroleum use. This could be made from just the stems once you have already harvested the seeds and leaves for other uses.

GARDEN

Alfalfa is a valuable green manure or cover crop as it can withstand winter frosts and will keep your empty vegetable beds weed free. The roots can extend down as far as 6m, bringing up nutrients from deep below the soil's surface and holding them in its foliage. These are then reincorporated into the soil when the alfalfa is dug into the top layers where it will rot and provide nutrients for the new crops. A covering of alfalfa will provide erosion control and reduce rainfall runoff, allowing more water to penetrate the earth than would happen on a bare patch of soil. It can be left to grow for more than one season, although the older it is the harder it will eventually be to dig back into the soil. When grown as a green manure it is usually dug back into the soil at any point between 3 and 24 months after sowing. If you choose to leave alfalfa growing for more than one season it would be beneficial to trim back the tops two or three times during the growing season. Add the tops to your compost or use as a mulch to effectively recycle the nutrients that are brought up into the foliage by the

deep roots whilst maintaining ground cover. Alfalfa helps to fix nitrogen in the soil for the coming crop but if this is your primary reason for using a green manure I would recommend using clover instead as it has a much greater ability to fix nitrogen. Using a green manure will not only help protect your soil but will also improve fertility, soil structure and increase the level of organic matter content. Rotate your alfalfa patch every couple of years so that all areas under cultivation get their deep resources mined and recycled.

Pollinated by bees, moths and butterflies, alfalfa attracts a large amount of beneficial wildlife to your garden.

It makes a good companion plant for fruit trees and grape vines.

MISCELLANEOUS

Alfalfa has been used as forage for grazing animals for over 1000 years. Allow animals to graze on it during spring and autumn. Horses especially seem to like it. Fed to cows it will help increase milk yield, while sheep and goats also benefit from having it in their diet. It can be cut up to 5 times a season to provide either hay or silage or simply grazed in situ.

The curling seed pods can make an interesting

addition to seasonal flower arrangements.

The seeds provide a yellow dye.

Alfalfa provides good bee forage from which you can obtain good quality honey.

Drinking juice made from alfalfa tops regularly will promote hair growth and improve the condition of your hair.

The stalks can be made into paper.

AMARANTH
(Amaranthus spp.)

THE WORD AMARANTH comes from the greek *amarantos* which translates as 'everlasting' or 'never-fading flower', and although not frost hardy you will end up with a perenial patch if you allow some of the seed to fall to the ground where they will germinate the following spring. It provided a valuable food for the Aztecs and other historic races in the Americas and has been domesticated for 1000s of years. These days it is grown as a food crop across the globe from Africa, Europe, the Indian sub-continent and Asia to the Americas where it's seeing a resurgence after falling out of vogue for literally hundreds of years. Despite its many uses it is most often grown for its seed which is often refered to as a grain.

VARIETIES

There are over 50 species within the amaranth genus. Some are grown primarily for their seed and others simply as ornamentals or forage crops for livestock. I have listed a small selection of the more common varieties here:

Love-lies-bleeding *(Amaranthus caudatus) is* a very decorative variety which can grow up to 2m high with a spread of 50cm in hot weather. It is drought tolerant, can produce up to 100,000 seeds on one plant and will survive in highly alkaline soils.

A. cruentus grows as tall as *A.*

caudatus and will tolerate acid soils. It is the variety most commonly grown for food use.

A. hybridus grows to a height of 1m and ripens early, making it useful in areas that suffer from early frosts or short growing seasons.

Prince of Wales Feather (A. hypochondriacus) grows to approximately 1.2m and produces prolific amounts of seed. It ripens late in the season so is better for areas that experience long summers or mild autumns.

A. tricolor has strikingly beautiful foliage and is often grown for its aesthetic qualities as an ornamental but also makes a tasty salad vegetable.

GROWTH HABITS

Amaranth is an annual and the different species have different characteristics, with flowers varying from a deep crimson to green and their height from 0.5-2.5m. It grows best in fertile, well drained soil, not tolerating waterlogged soils. It likes full sun but can also take partial shade and is drought resistant. It is advisable to plant it in situ as it does not transplant well. To sow sprinkle the seed over a fine, weed free soil and cover with a thin layer of soil in late May or early June. Thin seedlings to a spacing of around 15cm between plants to avoid overcrowding and to gain maximum yield. The plants mature ready for seed harvest within 75 days.

MAINTENANCE

Luckily amaranth does not suffer from any major disease problems and is very easy to grow. You may need to weed between seedlings while they are small but once they reach about 10cm in height they will begin to shade out weeds.

HARVESTING, PROCESSING AND STORAGE

Amaranth is not frost tolerant so be sure to crop before the first frosts arrive. Harvest as the seeds are starting to drop naturally. Cut the mature flower heads into a bowl and then sieve to separate off the seeds. The seeds are best stored in an airtight container in the fridge and used within 3-6 months. They have a high oil content and if not stored in this way may go rancid.

If collecting the flowerheads for their medicinal properties, collect as the flowers are opening. Hang the flowerheads to dry away from direct sunlight and store in an airtight container. Leaves collected for medicinal infusions can also be dried and stored in this way.

USES

FOOD

The seed itself is a very healthy addition to the diet and contains 14-16% protein, which is higher than any gluten free grain. It is also high in lysene, an important amino acid. It contains double the amount of calcium in cows' milk, ten times the amount of iron than the same quantity of white rice would provide and a high magnesium, potassium and phosphorus content. The seed is high in fibre, has a low carbohydrate content, is a good source of polyunsaturated fatty acids and vitamin A, C and E and on top of all that it is easily digested. Cook the seed and eat hot as an accompaniment to saucy dishes instead of rice or use cold to bulk out a salad. The flavour is rather bland so you may want to cook it in stock. You can also use it to thicken sauces, stews and soups. Porridge can be made with the seed. Try sweetening it with honey or dried fruit. It only takes 15-20 minutes to cook and has a slightly sticky texture, so be careful not to overcook or it will become rather mushy.

The seed can be sprouted and then added to salads and sandwiches. There is no need to pre soak the seed, just rinse regularly (every 8-12 hours) and within 2 or 3 days small, white tail like sprouts will have emerged. Don't let the sprout grow longer than the seed or they will become bitter. The sprouts remain crunchy and can be kept in the fridge for a couple of days if you want to save some for later.

Grind the seed in a coffee grinder to make a gluten free flour for use in baking, although it is best combined with other flours as alone it will be too crumbly. The flour can also be used to make flat breads and is used for making chappatis in Nepal.

The seeds can be lightly toasted to make a popcorn like snack that is traditionally sweetened with either honey or molasses.

The seeds can be fermented and brewed as beer. It is common to find this kind of beer, known as chicha, in Peru.

Cold press the seeds to obtain an oil that is high in linoleic acid and contains all of the essential amino acids. Do not cook with this oil, rather drizzle it over salads.

Young leaves can be eaten raw in salads but as the leaves get older they need to be steamed or cooked and can then be used like spinach. The leaves are more nutrient rich than spinach, having higher quantities of not only calcium and phosphorus but also iron.

The stalks can be steamed and

eaten like asparagus, stir fried or added to dhal and boiled. The younger stalks are more tender but older stalks will need peeling before eating and may become totally inedible as they become quite fibrous with age.

MEDICINE

Make an infusion from the flowers and use as a mouthwash to treat toothache and a drink to sweat out a fever. Leaves can be added to the flowers in an infusion and drunk to cleanse the blood, regulate the menstrual cycle, dry up excessive bleeding during menstruation and to calm diarrhoea. The infusion, once cooled, can be dabbed on the skin to dry up and bring relief from acne, skin wounds, weeping eczema, psoriasis and hives. Use the infusion as a mouthwash to soothe and repair mouth ulcers and sore or bleeding gums.

The seed contains tocotrienols, a form of vitamin E, so eating amaranth as a regular part of a healthy diet has the capacity to lower cholesterol.

Consuming the seed oil may benefit those suffering from hypertension and cardiovascular disease whilst giving the immune system a boost.

There are no reported cautions or contraindications for using amaranth medicinally.

FUEL

Dried stalks can be burned as a fuel for heating or be converted into cellulosic ethanol to fuel petrol engines (see p172).

GARDEN

They make beautiful ornamental plants, the taller varieties adding height and colour to the backs of your beds, whilst their foliage will crowd out weed growth below, making them a good plant for areas that are difficult to access regularly.

MISCELLANEOUS

The leaves can be used as pig forage and the seeds as chicken fodder.

The leaves can be turned into silage.

The red pigment in the flowers and foliage can be used as a red dye.

The seed oil can be used as a lubricant for machinery.

The oil contained in amaranth seed has a high squalene content, higher than has been found in any other plant. Squalene is an expensive and sought after ingredient used in skin cosmetics. On an industrial scale it is currently sourced from the livers of whales and sharks supplied by the whaling nations for significant financial gain. Extracting the squalene from amaranth seed oil on a large scale could potentially damage the income of those who exploit a legal loophole in the whaling ban, perhaps making whaling less viable as a commercial venture. This would hopefully have the knock on effect of helping to preserve these huge, yet graceful sea giants. Any takers?

BAMBOO

BAMBOO IS AN incredibly useful resource, having around 20,000 recorded uses. Across south east Asia many everyday items are made from bamboo. In Thailand, for example, chairs, tables, bridges, cooking utensils, flutes and even ashtrays are constructed from this plant. It's not just Asia, but the peoples of North and South America, Africa and even Australia have utilised and benefited from bamboo's versatility for centuries. Native peoples from the Cherokee to the high Andean dwellers of Columbia have known and celebrated the strong, pliable material, using it in a multitude of ways from mats, baskets, arrow stems, fencing and vegetable supports to shelter.

It is estimated that 1 billion people live in homes made from bamboo. That is roughly 1 in 7 people on this planet![1]. I have stayed in bamboo huts throughout Asia and the woven walls allow air to circulate freely, negating the need for air conditioning which its modern, concrete replacements require. It's also free passage for insects as they can come and go, as can huge geckos and lizards, once they have feasted on the annoying little mozzies that would love to be feasting on you. In the tropics where humid conditions prevail, air circulation is necessary or mould will form. Concrete soon grows ugly as it stains with black moisture trails and green streaks and requires a lot more energy to produce and remove. You can simply burn the bamboo walls once they have reached the end of their useful life which in itself can form the warming centre piece of a social occasion, after which the ash can be collected to feed potassium hungry plants in the garden.

The fastest growing terrestrial plant, bamboo is in fact a giant grass. It grows straight and tall with each long cane broken into sections by joints. These long stems or canes are known as culms. The culms taper towards the tip and are broadest at their base where the stresses are greatest. The culm walls are made of cellulose fibres and contain lignin, a complex chemical compound also found in wood which binds to cellulose fibres to harden and strengthen the cell walls. The outer walls contain up to 5% silica, providing additional hardness and strength. Inside each culm is a series of hollow chambers, the separation between each marked by noticeable 'nodes' which appear like circular ridges on the outside surface of the culm. It is also at these points that very fine branches adorned with narrow, elongated leaves separate off from the main stem. Each of the hollow compartments are separated at the nodes by a rigid internal membrane or diaphragm which gives strength to the overall structure, in effect preventing the length buckling in extreme conditions. Due to this segmented form if any

damage occurs to a culm it will only die back as far as the next node. According to Bell, the high-tensile longitudinal fibres of the bamboo culms, although set in a softer matrix, have incredible similarities to carbon fibre. These characteristics make bamboo, on a strength to weight basis, stronger than steel[2]. It is not surprising then to learn that bamboo is used as scaffolding throughout much of Asia.

Perhaps one of the reasons for bamboo's great success as a prolific grower across the globe may be its ability to adapt and make the best of its conditions. Plants growing outside their optimum niche soon become stressed and are out competed by plants more suited to the prevailing conditions; bamboo, however, will find a way to flourish.

VARIETIES

There are a great many varieties of bamboo that can be grown in temperate climates, each with individual characteristics and differences such as colour, diameter of culm or strength. Different varieties are suitable for different uses. Bamboos from the genus *Phyllostachys* do well in the UK climate and generally have large, tasty shoots and strong canes. Due to the relatively cool climate in the UK they rarely reach their potential height or girth upon these shores but may do so in other temperate regions that enjoy warmer summers. The greatest diameter a bamboo grown within the UK is likely to achieve is about 8cm.

Golden *(Phyllostachys aurea)*, also known as 'fish pole bamboo', is good for general purposes including hedges. It tends to zigzag slightly between nodes which can be used to its advantage in structures such as trellises. It grows up to a maximum of 8m tall with diameters ranging from 1-6.5cm, achieving the lower end of this range in the UK. It is hardy to -20°C (-4°F) and once established can occasionally tolerate drought conditions too.

Yellow-groove *(Phyllostachys aureosulcata)* grows to a height of 6-8m with a diameter of 2.5-3.5cm. Hardy to -22°C (-8°F), this species can become invasive in warmer climates.

Giant Timber *(Phyllostachys bambusoides)* is thick walled and provides a hardwood often used in construction and furniture making. They can reach a height of between 8 and 22m with a 2.5-15cm diameter. It is hardy to -15°C (5°F).

Sweet shoot *(Phyllostachys dulcis)* cannot tolerate drought and has rather weak canes, so is usually grown for the tasty shoots. It grows to a maximum height of 12m with a diameter of 7cm and is hardy to -20°C (-4°F).

Moso-chiku *(Phyllostachys edulis)* can be slow to establish, eventually reaching between 6 and 20m in height, with a diameter of 18cm. It likes a sunny spot but is hardy to -20°C (-4°F).

Big-node *(Phyllostachys nidularia)* grows to between 6 and 10m tall with a diameter of up to 4cm. It is hardy to -18°C (0°F).

Black *(Phyllostachys nigra)* is a beautiful black stemmed bamboo producing a durable wood most often used for furniture. It grows to between 7.5 and 15m tall with a 1.5-7.5cm diameter. It is hardy to -18°C (0°F).

(Phyllostachys nuda) grows up to 7.5m tall with a diameter of 3cm and is hardy to -26°C (-15°F).

Moso *(Phyllostachys pubescens)* produces quite a soft yet versatile wood and reaches heights of between 3.5 and 6m with diameters ranging from 5 to an incredible 18cm, most usually only achieving the lower end of this range in the UK. It makes a good screen or hedge.

Red Margin (*Phyllostachys rubromarginata*) has large inter node spaces of up to 40cm and the larger culms tend to bulge just above the nodes. It produces good quality wood with a height of around 9.5m and diameters ranging from 2.5-6cm. It is hardy to -20°C (-4°F).

Kou-chiku *(Phyllostachys sulphurea viridis)* reaches heights of between 4 and 15m, with a diameter of approximately 8.5cm. It is hardy to -20°C (-4°F).

Phyllostachys viridi glaucescens grows to around 10m with diameters of 4cm or greater and is hardy to -20°C (-4°F).

Vivax *(Phyllostachys vivax)* provides good quality wood and reaches 15m in height with a diameter of 5-9.5cm. It is hardy to -23°C (-10°F).

Phyllostachys is not the only genus that will grow well. Check out members of the following genera to find the characteristics you are looking for but note that not all species within each genus will be suitable for your own climatic niche, so be sure to check before making your choice:

Bashina spp.

Chimonobambusa spp. (tends to thrive in damp, shaded conditions with high humidity).

Fargesia spp. (general characteristics are wind tolerance and being very hardy).

Pleioblastus spp. (robust and can be vigorous spreaders).

Pseudosasa spp. (less invasive than many other running types).

Semiarundinaria spp. (good for windbreaks and hedges and relatively tall with most species averaging between 8 and 10m).

Shibataea spp. (much lower in height than many bamboos averaging between 50cm and 2m depending on species and slow to spread).

Thamnocalamus spp. (hardy and clump forming).

Yushania spp. (moderately invasive).

GROWTH HABITS

The distribution of bamboos is really limited only by extreme cold or regions of extreme aridity. Unlike the majority of grass species which only thrive in open conditions, bamboo is also well adapted to life in the forest as well as semi shade. Bamboo is by nature a woodland plant, thriving best in dappled shade where it is protected from prolonged cold spells. However, as long as the soil is rich in organic matter and there is a relatively regular supply of water they will find their way. Wild bamboo is prolific, especially in Asia and South America. Europe is the only continent where they really lack a presence in the wild, arguably a legacy of the last Ice Age. Surprisingly South and Central America have the greatest number of species, more even than those of Chinese origin. So with such a diverse range there is a bamboo species for almost every garden.

In tropical and equatorial regions clumping bamboo dominates, multiplying outward from dense, relatively circular clumps. Temperate bamboos are known as running bamboos, the underground rhizomes sending up growing shoots in all directions, sometimes at quite a distance from those which have already penetrated the earth's surface.

The growth rate of bamboos is incredible; the culms emerge from the earth already displaying their maximum diameter, reaching their maximum height within just two months. You can almost see them grow in front of your eyes and even in temperate regions the rate of growth can be up to 35cm in a single day! The rhizomes send up shoots in late spring and protected initially by overlapping leaves, the new culms often retain their protective sheaths around the base for the first couple of years. Once the shoot has emerged it grows telescopically.

Bamboo flowers infrequently,

anything between once every 30 and 120 years. Flowering often causes the plant to die back (although not necessarily the death) of the parent, although a healthy rhizome bed or the germination of new seedlings will allow the life of the bamboo to continue. If the bamboo has been grown in a container, through my own experience, after flowering they do tend to die. Do not feed your bamboo if it starts to look sickly or dead after flowering; just leave it to regenerate in its own time, perhaps giving just a little compost as a token of encouragement. Your bamboo may regenerate, although it could take up to a couple of years to show fresh signs of life, so discovering whether your bamboo lives on or not will depend on your patience and the pressure you may feel to fill the space with a more productive plant. Partial flowering may take place over the course of several years and if this has occurred it is much more likely that the bamboo will have continued to generate food for itself whilst flowering and will therefore have the strength to continue living after the flowering part of its cycle has passed. Planting a couple of varieties of bamboo will give you more security - if one flowers and dies you will still have the other. The infrequent flowering of bamboo is something of an enigma; other grasses which like bamboo are wind pollinated have a regular and precise flowering habit. It seems that as bamboo is such a vigorous grower from the root that perhaps the need for reproducing by seed has become almost redundant, hence the infrequency of flowering. When a certain bamboo does flower, large numbers of individuals of that type will do so simultaneously across the globe, an intriguing characteristic that ensures they do not self pollinate.

If your bamboo is flowering and you would like to start off new seedlings, collect the seed around 4-5 months after the fresh flowers produce yellow thread like pollen sacks. The seed are quick to lose viability, so plant them as soon as possible. Most varieties will take between a few days to several weeks to germinate but others can take a year, so be patient and keep them warm until they are looking strong.

If you want to propagate a new plant from a section of rhizome, first make sure it is a running type as clumping types will not grow by this method. Make sure that your section of rhizome has at least two active buds present, otherwise your segment will slowly die, unable to send up new culms. The best time of year to propagate from rhizome cuttings is early spring and it is important to nurture them, keeping them

warm and well watered until you have seen evidence of new growth. It will take around two years for your cuttings to really establish and start sending up decent sized culms.

Growing bamboo in pots or propagating by dividing the roots will have a dwarfing effect on their growth. It will take several years planted back in open soil before the new canes grow to full size.

If you have bought a bamboo and are planting it in the ground, loosen the soil in the hole you have prepared and add plenty of humus. This will help the structure of the soil, allowing for both moisture retention and adequate drainage. Give the bamboo a good soaking before planting it in the ground and cover with mulch; leaf mould, bark chippings or rotted animal manure are all good options and will help the soil stay warm and retain moisture. Do not use seaweed as bamboos are intolerant to salt. Make sure your bamboo receives plenty of water during its first year while it settles in.

MAINTENANCE

Thin out clumps in spring, leaving only the culms you would like to keep and remove unwanted shoots as they appear and dead or decaying culms at any time. A layer of mulch every couple of years will also benefit your bamboo, as will watering if you are going for a great height.

The culms grow from a dense network of underground rhizomes which form thick woven mats. Approximately 80% of this network is within the top 30cm of the soil. This thick mat can present a nightmare if you are trying to remove a stand of temperate running bamboos from your land. It is important then to somehow contain the rhizome mat by providing boundaries to growth, otherwise in favourable conditions bamboo is liable to become invasive. One benefit of the UK's relatively cool summers is that they never seem to run too far out of control, something I have witnessed in the warmer climate of Southern Spain. A simple solution is to confine your bamboo to a large container or alternatively, as the rhizomes will not cross a watercourse, its spread could be restricted by the presence of a waterway. Failing that you could create an intentional barrier. This would need to be 75cm deep and rise 5cm above the soil surface. Any small gap within the barrier will allow roots to penetrate, forming a gap wide enough for rhizomes to travel to the other side. A less labour intensive way to contain your bamboo would be to dig a shallow boundary which could be used as a path but would need to be approximately 30cm lower

than the surrounding ground surface. As the rhizomes spread horizontally close to the surface you will see any spread protruding over the edges of your sunken boundary and will be able to cut them, arresting their spread [3]. Bamboo can even travel under a tarmacked road and send up shoots on the other side, so careful planning of your bamboo positioning is paramount. Acquiring your bamboo from a specialist nursery will help you find the most appropriate bamboo for your requirements and climate and avoid the problems of overspreading (see resources for some specialist bamboo suppliers).

HARVESTING, PROCESSING AND STORAGE

Culms are ready for harvest within 3-5 years. Wear long sleeves and gloves when harvesting as silica crystals, which form on newly growing culms, can be abrasive, irritating and can scratch your skin. It is best to harvest bamboo in winter or early spring during its dormant phase. Harvest the older culms as they will have developed a greater strength than the younger ones. Each single culm lives for a maximum of around 8 years. Old culms tend to have a different colouration and potentially some scarring on the outer surface. They will also have a duller and less vibrant lustre than young ones. Dead culms can be used for many products, providing they are not damaged or rotten. Cut the culm straight across as close to ground level as you can manage. This will avoid potentially dangerous stumps hiding in the mulchy ground cover waiting to trip up some unsuspecting passer by. Remove any side branches and culm tops, known as 'brush'. These thin sections have various uses but rot slowly, so avoid adding them to your compost. If you are transporting the harvested culms to a different site for use, be sure to secure them firmly as being round and smooth they can be tricky and slide out of bundles.

Bamboo needs to be stored in a dry place and protected from the elements, otherwise it will absorb the moisture, especially if standing vertically on damp ground where it may rot. The colour will fade as it dries, most varieties (except nigra) becoming more or less uniformly buff coloured within 6 months, by which time it should have dried thoroughly and be ready for use. During the drying process the culms should be stored more or less upright which should help reduce the risk of damage caused by insects seeking any remaining plant sugars in the bamboo.

Any creations made from bamboo will age gradually as the silica degrades, leaving the outside surface pitted. The naturally waterproof surface of the culms will not easily absorb wood preserving preparations, although you can try to remove this outer protective layer before treating in an attempt to lengthen their lifespan. However, being organic the natural response to harvest, and therefore death, is a slow disintegration over time. This is ultimately unavoidable, yet the process holds an inherent degree of beauty as the bamboo slowly returns to dust and becomes soil once more.

If collecting leaves for their medicinal uses, do so during the growing season. Collect young stems for shavings during the summer. Dry the leaves and stem shavings away from direct sunlight and store in a cool, dark place.

When collecting shoots to eat, choose one that is no taller than 1m and take only the top 30cm. Make a lengthwise slit down the shoot and remove tough outer layers to expose the white and pale green edible flesh. Eat while fresh.

USES

Working with bamboo requires sharp tools as the silica on the outer skin of the culm will quickly dull the sharpness and can even damage the teeth of a saw. Don't forget to wear work gloves to protect yourself from sharp blades and splinters. If you plan to split your bamboo for use in a specific project it is worth noting that bamboo is easier to split when fresh, but allow for shrinkage as it dries.

In cooler, temperate regions such as the UK the size bamboo achieves, and thus its uses, are more limited than in the more humid sub tropical areas on the fringes of the temperate zone.

FOOD

The shoots of bamboo are highly nutritious and contain the eight essential amino acids that your body can only obtain from food. The fresh shoots of certain species can be eaten raw, such as those from *P. aurea, P. dulcis, P. sulphurea viridis* and *P. viridi glaucescens.* Other edible species include *P. castillonis, P. edulis, P. mitris* (whose shoots are reportedly especially tasty), *P. nigra, P. nuda, P. pubescens* and *P. quilioi.* All of these varieties, as is the case with the majority of bamboos, have rather bitter tasting shoots that will need boiling, draining and boiling again to remove the bitterness.

If you have a large stand of bamboo that flowers you can collect the seed, grind it into flour and use it as you would wheat flour, a small consolation perhaps if your favourite bamboo is

potentially dying. The flour can be made into a kind of porridge if cooked in water for about an hour. This provided an important addition to the diet in Malawi when maize crops failed[4]. Alternatively, and perhaps preferably, bamboo seeds can be brewed into beer.

Food can be cooked inside the culm of a large diameter bamboo. This is a technique I have seen used in Thailand to cook sticky rice. First cut a section of culm open at one end with an intact diaphragm at the bottom end. Wrap the rice in a large leaf (one that is non toxic as it will impart its flavour to the finished dish), place inside the culm and fill with water, stuffing a few leaves in the open end as a kind of plug. Place the base in hot coals at the edge of a fire and allow the water to boil for the usual rice cooking time and eat! This technique can be used to roast other foods, even fish or meat, although you may want to seek out a recipe rather than just experiment. Bamboo tubes can also be filled with food and placed in a steamer where they will impart a subtle hint of their distinctive flavour.

MEDICINE

Medicinal elixirs made from bamboo have been used for thousands of years in China and Indian Ayurvedic treatments.

Phyllostachys nigra is often used medicinally and an infusion of leaves will treat diarrhoea and vomiting, reduce fevers and kill intestinal worms whilst promoting and regulating menstruation. The cooled infusion can be applied externally to skin ulcers and used to clean wounds. Drink a decoction made from shoot shavings mixed with honey a maximum of twice daily for respiratory complaints, especially when coughs and phlegm are present.

Avoid using bamboo as a medicine if pregnant.

Clothing

The conical hats that come to mind in a stereotypical South East Asian rural scene are most often made from woven bamboo strips.

You can obtain really soft fabric from bamboo fibres. The fabric is naturally antibacterial, antifungal, breathable, thermo regulating, highly absorbent (so it carries sweat away from the skin) and relatively wrinkle resistant. The fabric is totally biodegradable, so once it has finished its useful life as a garment you can use it as mulch on the garden where it will eventually turn back to earth. Most of the bamboo clothes that you can buy in the store will have been heavily chemically processed in a way similar to the processing of wood chips and other cellulose

rich materials into rayon. You can, however, process it non chemically in a similar way to flax (see page 74) and hemp, although it will take longer to break down. The bamboo must first be crushed before being left to ret and during this process natural plant enzymes will break down the tough cell walls. Eventually the fibres can be combed out and spun into yarn ready for use. You can either knit with the yarn or weave it.

Fuel

Bamboo can be seasoned and burned, although it has only one tenth of the heating power and burn time of a hard wood such as oak, compensated perhaps by the fact it grows much more quickly. Split the culms before burning, otherwise the air between the nodes will expand on heating, eventually splitting the culms loudly with accompanying and potentially dramatic sparks. Little scraps of cane and brush can be used for kindling.

Bamboo can be made into charcoal that is three times more porous than wood charcoal, giving it a greater heating capacity. It is mainly used for cooking.

Building and Housing

Laminated bamboo board can be used as attractive and hard wearing flooring and as an alternative to wooden floor boards. The culms must first be split and pressed flat. The outer green layers and inner pith are then planed off before the sheets are dried in a kiln. Finally layer after layer are glued together and compressed[5].

You can make entire buildings and simple internal dividing walls either from long sections of culm set into a frame or by splitting the culms and using the lengths to weave large mats which are then also set into a frame.

Large diameter bamboo can be fashioned into guttering and basic water pipes. The hardest part of creating these is removing the internal diaphragms.

Household

If you have harvested bamboo with a large diameter you can make a whole number of very simple items for use within the home. Cut with a node at the bottom with the diaphragm still in place and finish to different lengths for uses such as a vase, a cup, a pen or utensil holder or a shallow dish for storing keys or jewellery.

Splitting a length of large diameter bamboo down the middle with a node at either end can provide a container with a multitude of uses such as a snack dish for dried fruit or nuts. Cutting a section with several nodes in will create a

dish or container with several compartments. Without nodes at either end you can make a small tray which is perfect for serving sushi.

Small lengths can be split and split again until you end up with some usable chopsticks. This may be a good way of honing your splitting skills and accuracy.

Sections of culm can be made into indoor and outdoor furniture such as tables, shelves, chairs, benches and slatted blinds or wine racks.

Bind several lengths of bamboo together to make a shower mat. The gaps will allow water to drain away. The lifespan will be shortened if the bamboo maintains contact with water over long periods of time, so remember to stand it against a wall to dry off once your shower is over.

Splitting bamboo thinly gives the raw material for weaving all manner of useful articles such as table mats and baskets.

Garden

Bamboo canes are an exceptionally useful resource in the garden and can be used as bean and pea supports, stakes to support tall or leggy plants or made into trellises to support vines and climbers. Small, split sections can be used for many seasons as plant labels using an indelible ink pen to write the name of the plant on the inside of the culm.

Due to its evergreen nature bamboo provides a year round living wind protection barrier, providing privacy and cutting out noise. Some leaves will drop in autumn but will be replaced by new growth the following spring. *Pseudosasa japonica* and *Fargesia nitida* are particularly wind tolerant while *Semiarundinaria fashiosa* and *Phyllostachys bissettii* are also both good to use in hedges.

The thick mat of underground rhizomes will provide a stabilizing influence on the soil and will help to reduce soil erosion, particularly useful on steep slopes that have been cleared of their natural vegetation.

Split a wide diameter bamboo down the middle, removing the diaphragms to get an open ended half tube. Fill with compost and plant your peas in it, then plant them out in the garden when they have got going by simply sliding them off the end and onto the patch of earth where they are to grow. This method is especially useful where slug damage is a problem, allowing the seedlings to get a head start before being exposed to slimy predators.

To make use of vertical space

in the garden when the soil surface is already fully packed, attach a selection of culms together by binding or screwing to make a long trough. Then line it to prevent soil falling through the gaps and from drying out too rapidly. Make ends from smaller off cuts and fill the trough with soil and plant up. You can make this type of structure in almost any size and support it with an A-frame, suspend it from a tree branch or attach it to a wall or fence.

Whilst growing bamboo always make time for a quiet moment of stillness when tending to these giant beauties. A stand of living bamboo has a wonderfully relaxing quality to it. Just sit in a bamboo grove and listen to the wind as it whispers through the leaves and you will feel its gentle, soothing nature. Creating a peaceful sanctuary to escape the worries of the world or a spot for meditation can be achieved with the planting of several bamboos with an area in the middle for seating, relaxation and reflection.

You could make fences and privacy screens for your garden. There must be a hundred different styles or ways of making such items. The screen could be a natural way to hide a less attractive bit of your house. Even the brush can be utilized, collected together and held in place by a frame of larger culms to create an effect similar to a reed fence. Gates can be made to compliment your fence or screen.

Bamboo can be used for handrails along the side of steps or slopes, either attached to a wall or supported by posts.

Bind short lengths of bamboo standing vertically (side by side) together and use as edging to delineate separate garden beds.

There are many more ways you can utilize bamboo canes; in garden construction, gazebos, pergolas, summerhouses and retaining walls to name but a few.

MISCELLANEOUS

Split the culms into strips from which you can weave baskets and even coffins for green burials.

The foliage of certain species such as *Arundinaria racemosa* can be used as cattle feed and the shoots can be used as pig forage, while the foliage and seed of some species can be used as poultry forage.

You can pulp the culms and make paper. First split the bamboo into the smallest you can manage, then weigh and add 15% of the dry weight in lye (or wood ash) to cold water. Add the bamboo and

cook up. You will need to boil it for many hours to thoroughly soften the bamboo and this process is rather smelly. After about 10 hours drain the bamboo and rinse it several times to remove all traces of lye. Pound it to mash up the bamboo further then put into a paper frame. Finally, press and hang it to air dry. Alternatively, you could use the sheaths that cover the new culms as they emerge from the ground as the raw material. Collect them in early summer when they have fallen from the culm or are easy to remove. Making paper with the sheaths will be much easier as they need less softening than the culms themselves.

Bamboo can also be made into umbrella handles, walking sticks and flexible flag poles.

You can make all kinds of musical instruments with bamboo, from wind chimes that provide a deep, clonking sound to Andean pan pipes, Himalayan and Thai flutes, basic didgeridoos and much more. In Malacca, Malaysia they pierce the culms of still living and growing bamboo so that they produce gentle notes as the wind blows through them[6].

Short lengths of bamboo can be lashed together to make rustic crates.

Small bridges, rafts and fishing rods can all be made from

bamboo.

In addition to all the practical uses bamboo also provides a much higher level of carbon sequestration than trees, at approximately 13.6 kg/m² compared to trees at 3.5 kg/m², whilst producing 35% more oxygen than trees[7]. This makes it a good choice if you are planting up an area to ease your carbon footprint conscience.

The list really is endless and is limited only by the size your bamboo can achieve, your imagination and handiwork skills.

NOTES

1.Doug Bancorn *"Bamboo is destroying our planet"* Green Earth News, August 30, 2009, online version.

2. Michael Bell, *The Gardener's Guide To Growing Temperate Bamboos* (David & Charles Publishers, 2000), 19.

3. Ibid., 54.

4 .George Ntonya *"Hunger Takes Toll In Salima"* The Malawi Nation, November 12, 2005, online version.

5. Carol Stangler *The Craft & Art of Bamboo* (Lark Books, 2001), 17.

6. Michael Bell, *The Gardener's Guide To Growing Temperate Bamboos* (David & Charles Publishers, 2000), 24.

7. Doug Bancorn *"Bamboo is destroying our planet"* Green Earth News, August 30, 2009, online version.

BANANA
(Musa spp.)

BANANA IS PERHAPS an interesting choice to include as being a tropical plant it will rarely produce mature fruit, certainly in the UK, unless it is carefully nutured in a glass house that is either heated or up against a south facing wall in a sheltered position. There is, however, so much more to the banana than its fruit alone and as different varieties are being bred for marginal climates and record high temperatures are being reached more often, why not experiment with something more exotic? I had considered including avocado or papaya, two other amazing tropical plants that have varieties bred to survive in more temperate climates, but I think banana remains the easiest to experiment with at this point. Another reason for the inclusion of banana is that I don't believe we should live feeling we are missing out on the tropical treats we grew up with and yet the guilt factor builds with the ever growing carbon footprint and our consciousness of it. The solution seems obvious; find a tropical delight that has been bred to survive in climates beyond its natural range and experiment to see what you can achieve with a little extra care and attention. You may be surprised and at least you will have fun trying.

Bananas are native to South East Asia and when ripe the fruits can vary in colour from yellow to purple and red.

Evidence of banana cultivation

49

going back at least 7000 years has been found in Papua, New Guinea. Commercially only one or two hybrids provide the majority of the fruit we find in supermarkets worldwide, Cavendish being the most popular. These are uniformly yellow when ripe and have no viable seed. In many parts of the tropics green bananas or plantain provide a staple. They are cooked in a similar way to potatoes, providing huge numbers of people with a valuable source of carbohydrates.

Varieties

Musa basjoo is a root hardy banana from Japan that will grow outside in the UK. The seedy fruits are edible, although this genus is most often grown for its strong fibres rather than its fruit. It will tolerate temperatures of -5°C (23°F) or -20°C (-4°F) with mulch and incredibly it has been reported to survive temperatures as low as -29°C (-20°F). It can grow to a height of almost 3m in the UK.

Musa acuminata 'Chinensis' will fruit after a couple of years if kept warm.

Musa dwarf cavendeshii – there are several types of *cavendeshii,* some only attaining 1.2m while others reach 2.4m. Topped up regularly with plenty of manure and grown in a

conservatory or heated greenhouse/polytunnel with a minimum temperature of 18°C (64°F), they will produce edible fruit after 3 years.

Musa dwarf rajapuri/Musa dwarf orinoco are also a better bet for fruit than *Musa basjoo.* The orinoco reaches around 1.8-2.4m in height.

Musa sikkimensis is hardy and can be grown outside with protection. It will grow to a height of between 3 to 4m and has attractive red tinged leaves which are tougher than other varieties and so will not shred so easily in the wind.

Musa 'Williams hybrid' will tolerate mild frosts with protection. It can reach 2-3m in height and produces large fruit.

Beware when choosing a variety as you will find *Musella lasiocarpa* touted as one of the world's hardiest bananas. It is an attractive ornamental, but not a banana, so will never bear the edible fruit you may be hoping for.

Growth Habits

Bananas are not trees but herbaceous perenials of the *Musaceae* family. They prefer light shade in a sheltered position with a rich, moist soil which can be translated as add plenty of compost and water regularly. The giant leaves are easily shredded in the wind, so a protected site is essential. Bananas will tolerate neither drought, waterlogging nor salty soils. Be extra vigilant when growing in a pot not to let your banana dry out or sit in water. Their natural preference is for light shade but full sun is preferable in temperate regions. Varieties which grow outside in this climate really appreciate any extra warmth they can get and planting against a south facing wall or even beside a cement or tarmac path will beneficially affect their microclimate. Plant in a good sized hole about 0.6m deep by 0.9m wide and back fill with rich compost high in organic matter.

Many varieties contain seed unlike the mass produced culitvars. When fresh the seed will germinate easily, however they lose viability rapidly and so rarely germinate when purchased. Offsets or corms are more reliable and can be obtained from specialist nurseries (see resources). These must be grown in pots and treated with care until they are large enough to be planted out into the earth. They will always have more chance of producing edible fruits if grown under cover in a conservatory, greenhouse or polytunnel. In the wild bananas most regularly reproduce from suckers which are sent up from the base in spring. Allowing the suckers to grow takes energy away from the original plant, thus reducing the chances of it flowering and fruiting. It therefore makes sense to remove the majority of them. If you do so, keep some of the root attached and pot them up which should lead to the successful propagation of a new plant. Make sure any new plant has well established roots, enough to fill a 2 litre container, before planting it back into the earth.

It takes between 10-15 months for a stem to flower, each stem producing just one flowering bud and a long, spiralling bunch of bananas. Only the first few hands will develop into fruit, the later emerging inflorescences being sterile and dropping off. After flowering the stem will naturally die back and be replaced by one of the suckers growing at the base. Remove the stem once the fruit has been produced so that it can be used before it starts to decompose. This will also ensure that all the nutrients coming from the roots go into the new sucker(s). A banana may last 25 years or more if allowed to continue growth through its suckers in this way.

If you are hoping to grow fruit, space your banana plants at about 2.5m, otherwise 1m should be plenty. Your plant will grow between April and September, stopping completely during the coldest months. If your banana is getting too tall for the space you have available, cut the stem to the required height and new leaves will miraculously emerge.

Some varieties are really tough. *Musa basjoo* will survive outside even when the soil is frozen to a depth of 30cm as long as you cut it down to ground level in the autumn and cover it with a thick mulch of straw. The subsequent summer will need to be long and warm if it is to fully recover and flourish, but in a good spot it will grow back to full height in a single season.

MAINTENANCE

If you are growing outside, winter protection is a must to keep your plants alive through the coldest months. The most important part to protect is the roots as if they get damaged you will lose your plant. Simply piling up a large mound of fallen leaves or straw around the base should work well. Leave the trunk intact or cut it down to a size that is easily covered, say 0.9m. This will work in all but the most exposed locations where you would be better off cutting to ground level. Any sections of stem you leave in place will need protection. Horticultural fleece or hessian are the most straightforward options or alternatively, use large tubes, perhaps chimney liners, placing them over the

stems and stuffing with straw. Make sure that whatever you use allows air to circulate and moisture to evaporate or you may end up with a mouldy mush come spring time. If any leaves remain unprotected, remove them at the first sign of frost damage. Remove the covering once the danger of heavy frost has passed. If it seems that despite your best efforts your banana has not survived the winter, cut it back to ground level and give it some time. It may regenerate from the root with a little prayer and a few encouraging words.

Virus and disease are unlikely to affect small scale home production outside of the tropics. The main threat in the temperate zone is root rot due to prolongued cold and wet conditions.

Mulch around the base of the stem to keep competition from grass and weeds to a minimum. Feed with potash during the growing season to improve the chances of producing fruit.

HARVESTING, PROCESSING AND STORAGE

In the tropics bananas will produce fruits all year round but here the fruits tend to appear late in the summer, stay on the plant over winter and plump up and reach ripeness the following year. Realistically fruit is only likely to reach maturity when grown in a heated space under glass. Once your plant has produced fruit big enough to harvest, cut off the whole fruiting section and hang it to ripen in a warm shaded place, or simply remove one hand of fruit at a time as they ripen. Once all the fruit has been removed, harvest the stem for other uses leaving one (the largest) sucker to grow on to maturity.

Sap from the stem stains, so wear gloves and old clothes when harvesting or processing the stems.

USES

Food

The bananas produced will often be very small, green and inedible in the UK climate. It is not unknown, however, to actually get some to mature. If you do manage to grow some large and ripe enough to eat, be careful of your teeth when tucking in as they will most likely contain hard seeds. Don't be put off by the size: if they ripen fully these small fruits are much sweeter and more tasty than their larger, blander supermarket cousins. High in potassium and carbohydrate, bananas are a great energy fix and useful when taking part in an all day activity as they replenish electrolytes and give a slow, sustained release of energy. If your bananas remain green, try frying or prepare them as you would plantains, adding them in chunks to stews and curries. Bananas are well known for being a great addition to smoothies and milkshakes, giving them a lovely thick texture but if blending or otherwise processing your own bananas, remove the seeds first.

If you can get bananas to mature and ripen and you are suddenly overwhelmed with a glut, remove the skins and freeze them. One option is to insert a stick into the base of your banana and dip it into melted chocolate before freezing. When you are ready for a treat, remove from the freezer and eat while still frozen like an ice pop. Alternatively, you can make a frozen dessert by placing the frozen bananas through a good quality juicer with the blanking plate on. Banana can also be preserved by drying, either in the sun, at a low temperature in the oven or a dedicated dehydrator (but keep the temperature at no more than 40°C (105°F) to ensure the enzymes remain intact). You can slice them into chips, quarter them lengthwise or puree and spread thinly to create fruit leather. Keep testing as it will take up to 24 hours for them to be ready. If you prefer to eat them hot, slice the banana skin while fresh and slip in a few chunks of chocolate, cover with kitchen foil and place in the hot coals of a fire for 10 minutes or so. Remove and eat your warm, melted chocolate and banana mash straight from the skin with a spoon. Alternatively, you can bake with sweet, ripe bananas. They make fantastic banana bread and can be added to cake, cookie and muffin recipes.

The ripe fruits can be fermented into an alcoholic beverage which is popular in Central and Eastern Africa.

If your warm season is too short and you cannot get your fruits to ripen then fear not. You will still be able to enjoy the delights of the unopened banana flower as it is edible. Remove the tough, outer layers then slice it very finely as you would a white cabbage for coleslaw and sprinkle it raw over stir fries, noodle soups, coconut milk curries or salads. You do not have to use the whole flower in one go as it will store in the fridge for a few days. Some people recommend removing all of the purple outer layers and the black pistils from the white flowers inside before using it to reduce bitterness.

The stem core is also edible. Remove the fibrous outer layers (there will be more of them on older stems) then chop the remaining core finely and soak it in buttermilk or salt water for a couple of hours. Drain and rinse then add it to stir fries, soups, dhals, curries or use it raw in salads. New shoots or suckers when removed from the base of the stem can be roasted and eaten.

MEDICINE

Juice the core of the banana stem and drink a glass in the morning and evening to help treat kidney and gall stones whilst providing a kidney cleanse.

Eating bananas regularly can act as a preventative medicine against the development of some cancers, notably breast and colorectal. The potassium content can help regulate blood pressure and is vital for the healthy functioning of nerves and muscle tissue. Bananas contain tryptophan which is converted to seratonin in the body which helps you relax and improves mood. They also contain B vitamins which help calm the nervous system and fibre which will help keep you regular.

Rub the inside of a ripe banana skin on mosquito bites to help reduce swelling and itchiness.

Eating banana flower will help cleanse the blood.

There are no reported cautions or contraindications for using banana parts medicinally.

CLOTHING

The long fibres found in the stem can be used to make a luxuriant soft fabric that can breathe and absorb moisture whilst also being quick to dry. This makes it especially comfortable to wear in hot climates or when exerting yourself and sweating. The fibre from the outer stem is the most coarse, getting finer with each layer inwards. The fibres are roughly separated and boiled in a lye solution for several hours before being rinsed thoroughly and dried. They are then combed to separate them further and spun. Keep the fibres moist when spinning and weaving by occasionally spraying with water from a plant mister as the yarn will snap if it gets too dry. If you have no facilities for weaving, try knitting with the yarn. Once your garments have worn out they can be used as mulch in the garden where they will slowly biodegrade, adding organic matter back to the earth.

FUEL

Waste from banana plantations can be digested anaerobically to break down the plant organisms. It will then produce methane (biogas). This is currently being run as a pilot scheme in Queensland, Australia to check its commercial viability. The idea is to power farm machinery and tractors from the natural gases produced.

Briquettes can be made from the discarded parts of the banana plant and used as a fuel source. The technique was developed by Joel Chaney, a PhD student at Nottingham University and has massive implications for parts of Africa where fuel wood is scarce and other sources of fuel are limited. The briquettes are an ideal alternative to wood fuel and are made by mashing up the leaves and skins, mixing them with the sun dried stems and compressing them into a brick before baking at 105°C (221°F) to dry them (this can be done in the sun in hot climates over a longer period). The briquettes can then be burned as an alternative to wood for heat or on your barbecue to cook with[8].

BUILDING AND HOUSING

The large leaves can be dried and lain thickly over beams then lashed to them for a rustic roofing solution. I have seen this done in the tropics but assume that it would be pretty lightweight and would most likely rot over the course of a long, wet winter. If you live in a relatively dry place why not give it a go on a shed or lean to in the garden? In the tropics this style of roof can withstand monsoon conditions but I should imagine it would require regular checks and repairs if you need the space below to be free from drips when the rain does fall.

HOUSEHOLD

The leaves can be used as disposable, or rather compostable, plates. They can also be used to wrap or cover food while it is being steamed or barbecued, imparting a subtle flavour to your meal whilst keeping it moist.

Yarn obtained from the processed fibres can be woven into place mats and table cloths.

GARDEN

In the garden a few banana plants can give architectural structure and a hint of tropical paradise.

Once your plant has passed its best you can cut the stem into small sections and it will decompose rapidly, adding bulk to your compost or organic matter to the soil if you add it as a mulch layer.

If you have several banana stems growing in a grove, any discarded leaves or chunks of stem can be thrown into the middle providing mulch and nutrients for the other stems. In essence this becomes a self mulching system much as it would when left to its own devices in the wild.

MISCELLANEOUS

Bananas are humectants, meaning they promote the retention of water. In addition they are naturally moisturising which makes them a great ingredient in homemade skin care treatments. For a moisturising face pack simply mash a ripe banana (or a few depending on size) and cover your face. Leave it in place for 10 minutes before rinsing off. You can also use banana in hair treatments. Try mashing ripe banana and combining it with a nourishing oil such as hemp for a deep conditioning and moisturising treatment for dry hair. Massage the mush into your hair and scalp, cover with clingfilm (plastic wrap) and leave in place for 30 minutes before rinsing off and washing with a mild shampoo.

A ripe banana placed in a paper bag with an unripe avocado will speed up its ripening due to gasses emitted by the banana.

When you peel an under ripe banana you will notice a slightly sticky substance collecting on the broken surface of the peel. This substance can also be collected from the stem and makes an effective adhesive.

Banana fibre can be pulped and made into paper.

The fibrous outer covering of

the stem can be peeled off and left to dry in strips. These strips can then be split further to produce a fine but rough string like fibre which can be used around the house and garden in a similar manner to regular garden twine.

The fibre from banana leaf can be woven and made into baskets or coffins for green burials.

Huge research projects, such as the €1million Badana project, carried out by Queens University Belfast, are ongoing to study the viability of converting the 'waste' from plantations (mainly stems that have fruited) into rotationally moulded plastics. The idea is to sandwich banana fibre between thin layers of plastic, reducing the amount of polyethylene used whilst strengthening the finished products[9].

NOTES

8. *"Scientists Produce Fuel Using Parts of The Banana Plant"* www.promusa.org, June 2009.

9. *"Banana Plants May Be Used in Production of Plastc Products"* Queens University Belfast, October 9, 2009, online (www.sciencedaily.com).

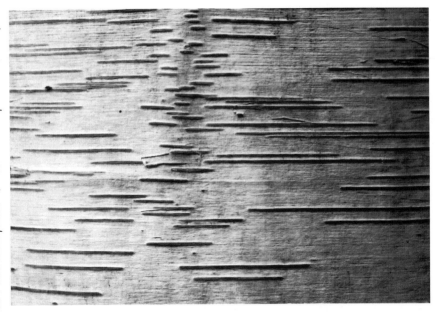

BIRCH
(Betula spp.)

BIRCH IS KNOWN as the mother tree and is often seen as a symbol of rebirth and renewal. In the Celtic tradition it symbolises new beginnings and young love. Birch is a venerated tree with a huge quantity of associated myth and folklore, from cultures as diverse as the Ancient Greeks and Scandinavians to the people of Canada's first nations. In the UK birch is used in traditional celebrations throughout the year. A birch log is burned on winter solstice to symbolise the end of the old year and to bring in the new and birch is also used at Beltane, the spring festival, to make a maypole which is danced around as a symbol of fertility. It is said that a house adorned with birch will protect the dwellers from lightening, the evil eye, gout and barrenness.

Birch produces a tough, relatively dense, hardwood that is straight and fine grained, ranging in colour from golden brown to whitish, which when polished has a beautiful, satin-like sheen. The distinctive bark has a multitude of uses and due to its high oil content is waterproof and exceptionally enduring, surviving on a fallen tree as an empty tube long after the wood of the trunk and branches has rotted away. It contains natural chemicals that are resistant to fungal decay, lengthening the useful life of the bark further. Birch is easily recognised by its bark, silver birch especially where the bark peels off easily in layers, like thin white sheets of paper.

A mummified man named Oetzi, dating back to approximately 3300BC, was found on the Austrian-Italian border in 1991. Amongst his possessions were two birch bark containers, while his weapons were attached to their shafts with birch tar[10] showing that the versatility and importance of birch as a material has been recognised and utilised for thousands of years.

VARIETIES

Downy birch (*Betula pubescens)* grows to a height of 18m, with a spread of 10m.

Paper birch *(Betula papyrifera),* known as canoe birch, is native to central north eastern North America and grows to a height of 27.5m with a trunk diameter of up to 60cm.

Silver birch *(Betula pendula)* can reach a height of 30m.

White birch *(Betula alba)* grows to a height of 15m with a trunk diameter of 30cm. The bark peels off in papery strips.

GROWTH HABITS

Birch will grow well in most soils, even poor quality acidic soils. Downy birch will tolerate very poorly drained soils.

Birch is a natural coloniser of deforested land. It has a strength and pioneering spirit to it and a corresponding ability to grow further north and at greater altitudes than most other trees. The fallen leaves, high in nitrogen and phosphorus, will condition the soil whilst gradually raising the pH level where they fall, helping to make acidified land become more suitable for other species to follow. It can establish itself in areas of very shallow soil, needing a depth of only 30cm. It is also particularly frost hardy, even growing in permafrost areas of Alaska. This property makes it a good species to grow around more frost sensitive trees as protection. Birch will not tolerate salt laden winds coming off the sea.

The leaves are amongst the first to appear in early spring, punctuating the muted browns and greys of late winter with the first splashes of fresh green. The small leaves cast only a light shade, allowing other plants to grow beneath its canopy. It is, however, intolerant of much shade itself and so will be difficult to establish in a shady spot, prefering an open, sunny aspect.

Birch grows rapidly during the first 25 years or so of its life, gradually slowing down after that. The trunk does not achieve a particularly large diameter, certainly in the UK where anything over 30cm would be rare. Birch is relatively short lived, living to a maximum age of around 200 years but more commonly reaching only 70 or 80. These characteristics, however, make it a good tree for coppice as long as it is initially cut when young (within the first 10-20 years). It will grow happily and rapidly in the newly opened up areas, producing faggots in just a 3 or 4 year cycle and wood for turnery or fuel in a 15-25 year rotation.

Pollinated by wind, birch will reproduce by seed, but also vegetatively by the growth of buds at the base of the tree which will put forth a number of shoots. The shoots will naturally thin out as some become stronger, growing more vigorously, whilst others die back. Birch is easily propagated with soft wood cuttings. Find a healthy looking tree in spring and take a newly grown shoot around 15-20cms long that has no buds or flowers. Make a straight cut at the base 1cm below a leaf node, remove any leaves from the bottom half of the shoot leaving just one or two at the growing tip and wrap in damp tissue to keep it moist. Soak it in a rooting hormone before potting. Use a 50:50 mix of compost and sand, make an 8cm deep hole with a pencil and insert the cutting, firming up around the base. Keep your cutting warm and moist and it will

soon produce roots and can be planted out within a year. Whether growing from seed or propagating from cuttings, be careful when eventually planting out as just 20 minutes of bare root exposure can kill a tree.

MAINTENANCE

If you are growing birch within a forest it will benefit from some thinning of the surrounding trees to allow it the light it needs to thrive. There are few pests and diseases that really impact on birch but browsing animals, especially deer, rabbits and squirrels are regularly the worst offenders, so depending on your site you may consider protection, certainly in the early years. Honey fungus, if present, will infect and kill a tree, so be vigilant and at the first signs of infection remove and destroy the tree to prevent its spread.

HARVESTING, PROCESSING AND STORAGE

The leaves can be collected for medicinal uses either when still in bud or when newly opened. Leaves and bark collected for medicinal properties can either be used fresh or dried at room temperature away from direct sunlight and then stored in an airtight container ready for later use.

The outer bark will begin to peel naturally with age, but be mindful that the bark protects the tree from insects and disease and so, if possible, it is always best to use bark from branches that have been removed or sections of trunk from a cut tree. It will, however, heal when damaged and so bark can also be collected from living sections of the tree as long as it is only small strips and not a ring of bark encircling the entire trunk as this will kill the tree. Bark should be collected in the summer months, mid summer being the best time (late June, until early July) as this is the time the tree is least likely to be damaged by this activity and the bark will be easiest to peel. There are many factors which will determine the characteristics of the bark such as the age of the tree and the position on the trunk. You will most likely only learn which bits of bark are right for you with experience and sensitivity to the tree. Be careful to make only a shallow cut (approximately 0.5cm) into the bark when harvesting it from a live tree and avoid cutting into the inner bark or the wood itself.

If you have harvested bark for craft purposes, roll it to store until use. Roll with the outside inwards, the opposite way to how it was on the actual trunk or alternatively, you can store it flat. Whilst in storage it must be kept dry and out of direct sunlight. If it has gone brittle during storage, soak it in warm water or steam it over boiling water before use to restore softness and flexibility. If planning on weaving with strips of bark it may help to apply a little beeswax before starting as this will moisten the bark. In addition the application of beeswax will impart a richer colour to the strips and lubricate them, protecting your fingers.

Birch tar (also known as pitch) can be extracted from the bark. There are several steps to the process but it is relatively simple. First collect up strips of bark. They don't need to be freshly harvested as the bark will retain its oil long after parting from the living tree. Next you will need to find a circular tin such as a biscuit tin with a lid. Make a hole in the bottom of this tin - the diameter of a pen should do it. Then roll all your lengths of bark tightly together and place them in the tin, squidging extra bits of bark in any gaps. Make sure the rolled sections are standing upright in the tin so that the oil can run off and down unobstructed through the hole. Next you will need a much smaller tin, such as an old baked bean can. Make sure it is clean and bury it in a snug fitting hole in the ground. Place the larger tin over this, making sure the hole in the larger tin is centrally lined up over the smaller tin and with the base of the big tin flush with the top of the smaller one. Place the lid firmly on at this point. Build up a little earth around the bigger tin once in place to be sure it does not move around during the next stages of processing. Next build a fire over and around the large tin. Extreme heat will build up in the tin and oil from the bark will be extracted, distilling in the smaller tin. The process will take a couple of hours, so make sure your fire is burning well for this amount of time.

At the end of the process the large tin will contain the charred remains of the bark and the smaller tin will have runny oil inside. Do not expose the small tin to naked flame as the contents and their vapours are extremely flammable and you could quickly burn all your valuable tar. Depending on what you are using the tar for it can be applied in this runny state or gently reduced by allowing it to bubble away next to the coals of the fire. As it is flammable avoid exposure to any naked flame. Eventually it will become more sticky and you will be able to collect the cooling tar by rolling the end of a stick around in the can. You will end up with something that resembles a lollipop. Store it until needed. To use it expose it to a flame for a couple of seconds so the tar becomes pliable and use it straight away as it will cool and stiffen again quickly. Allow your lollipop to cool and store

it again until you need to use some more.

If you are collecting seed so that you can propagate some seedlings, they normally ripen around September and can be collected from then until November.

Sap is collected in spring as it is rising and the timing of this will depend on your location and how early the leaves appear. It needs to be tapped before the appearance of the leaves (and this can be as early as March or as late as May). Choose a relatively mature tree with a trunk diameter of no less than 20cm. Make a hole in the trunk on the sunny side of the tree with a hand drill or a sharp knife. The diameter need only be 1-1.5cm and approximately 2cm deep. Angle the hole slightly upwards into the trunk as this will facilitate the flow of sap down and out. The sap will start to drip out and this can be quite fast. The best way to collect it is to push a drain into the hole in the trunk and you can make a drain by getting a small stick and gouging a channel to the end. When you push this into the hole make sure the channel is on the top side and either hang a collection vessel from the drain or position one on the ground below. This could be a jar or an old plastic container. You may be suprised at how quickly this fills, so keep checking. A mature tree can produce 1-1.5 litres a day. Do not collect more than 5 litres per tree per season. When you are done, remove the drain and make a snug fitting plug to push back into the hole to seal it, protecting the tree from permanent damage, disease or insect infestation.

USES

FOOD

The young leaves can be eaten fresh and are high in vitamins A, B1, B2, C and E.

Drinking the fresh sap as it comes out is a well known tonic that will keep you vibrant and youthful. The sweet sap is made up of glucose and fructose and can be evaporated after tapping to form a sweet, sticky mass, once rather confusingly known as maple syrup! Birch syrup has a rather dark colour and a taste not dissimilar to molasses. You can make wine from the sap and a basic recipe is to add 200g of sugar and a dash of wine maker's yeast to a litre of sap. Cover it with a breathable cloth and leave it at 22°C (72°F) to ferment for 4-5 weeks before bottling[11]. Recipes are also available for specialities such as birch beer, champagne and even root beer.

MEDICINE

Silver birch is the type most often used for its medicinal qualities. Both the leaves and bark contain salicylates, pain-relieving and anti-inflammatory components that are the active ingredients in the drug aspirin.

The bark, leaf buds, leaves and sap are all used in medicinal preparations, although it is the leaves that are most commonly used. Birch is anti-inflammatory, antiseptic, astringent, diuretic, laxative and provides pain relief. A leaf infusion will bring relief from joint problems such as arthritis and gout. Regularly drinking the infusion will act as a preventative against attacks of gout as it helps decrease levels of uric acid, elevated levels of uric acid being the cause of this painful condition. The leaves can bring relief from rheumatism, kidney and bladder complaints such as cystitis and some skin conditions including psoriasis and eczema. Drinking one cup of the infusion each morning before breakfast will help clear up acne outbreaks. Use the leaf infusion as a mouthwash to help speed the healing of mouth ulcers and sores. The leaves can alternatively be juiced. Drink 10ml twice daily or make a tincture from them. Use 1ml up to 3 times daily. The leaves can also be used fresh as a poultice on painful or inflamed joints and will bring relief from arthritis.

If you drink the fresh sap or sap wine you will benefit from birch's anti-inflammatory and diuretic properties.

Recent medical research has isolated compounds within birch bark that can kill cancer cells without undesirable side effects. The research is ongoing. The bark can be used in a number of ways, one of the most simple being to peel a small section and place the damp, inner side down on painful and aching muscles to provide pain relief. You can also make a decoction from the bark and either add it to your bath water or apply it to your skin with cotton wool. Both of these methods will provide pain relief and help to dry up and heal moist skin irritations including stubborn sores, open wounds and minor burns.

Birch tar can be made into a salve and applied externally to treat skin conditions including warts, psoriasis and eczema.

Use birch with caution if you are sensitive to aspirin.

CLOTHING

Shoes can be woven from birch bark and their use was widespread in pre-industrial Finland where it was documented that they tended to wear through after a walk of around 16km[12]. They may not last long but at least they are cheap and easy to repair if you are in the vicinity of a birch tree!

FUEL

Thin stips of peeled bark work as excellent firelighters, burning easily and well and getting even a reluctant fire off to a good start. Birch can be used to make charcoal and seasons ready for burning as fuel wood after 12 months. It makes a good fuel wood, smells pleasant when burning and will burn unseasoned if you have nothing else. Once seasoned you may want to burn it with slower burning woods such as oak or elm as it does tend to burn very quickly on its own.

BUILDING AND HOUSING

It can be milled into planks for use as attractive and durable flooring.

The wood can be made into plywood and boardwood.

The waterproof bark can be made into roof tiles.

HOUSEHOLD

Small pieces of the wood can be made into kitchen utensils such as wooden spoons, spatulas and replacement handles for old utensils.

The wood can be used to make fine furniture such as chairs with turned legs and struts.

Birch can be made into a beautiful and hardwearing veneer for furnishings.

Beautiful bowls can either be carved or turned from a chunk of birch.

Small branched pieces can be used as hooks on walls or doors for hanging coats and suchlike.

Rustic furniture can be made from medium branches and depending on how rustic you want it to look you could leave the bark on. You could even make picture frames to match your rustic chairs!

The bark has been extensively used throughout history to make drinking cups, ladles and even makeshift cooking pots. If you want to make any of these items, be aware that you will need to seal the joints and seams with resin or birch tar to make them watertight.

Strips of inner bark can be used to weave coasters, place mats, knife sheaths and chopstick holders.

You can also make boxes with or without lids and trays from sections of bark.

GARDEN

Use the thin branches for bean poles and milled or cleft sections of trunk for fence posts. Unlike the bark the wood itself is not particularly resistant to decay, so if used outside as fence posts it will need treating with a preservative.

Collect the fallen leaves in autumn, place them in a black bag and moisten with water, then leave for a couple of years by which time they will have formed a dark, nutritious leaf mould that you can use to enrich your beds.

Birch trees support a diversity of fauna, especially birds who feed on the seeds and buds, making it a valuable host species.

If you have a garden that is perpetually soggy then planting birch will help to dry the soil.

Birch is a good choice for hedging and shelter belts as it can tolerate windy conditions.

A small section of harvested birch trunk or branch can be used as a habitat for ladybirds and other beneficial insects. Drill holes into the wood at an upward angle to provide warm and safe places for insects to live and breed. Cover with a sweet chestnut shingle or similar which will protect the central wood from rotting too quickly. The bark itself will protect the outsides. Attach to a post and leave in a quiet part of your garden for the insects to find.

MISCELLANEOUS

To make an antiseptic hair lotion that will both condition

the hair and stimulate hair growth make two tinctures (see p179), one from birch leaf, the other from birch buds. Add a teaspoon and a half of each to a jug of water and add a few drops of essential oil for fragrance (rosemary is a good choice as it is also deeply conditioning and stimulates hair growth). Mix together then pour over clean hair before drying. If you have collected birch sap you can make a hair rinse by adding a spoonful of the sap to a jug of water, stirring thoroughly then pouring over clean hair and leaving to dry. This will provide your hair with a deeply nourishing and conditioning treatment.

To make a deep conditioning hair shampoo make a strong infusion of birch leaves and buds in a litre of distilled water, add to 150g of grated castile soap and follow the instructions on p140 for nettle shampoo.

The leaves can be fed to cattle.

Leaves harvested in spring make a creamy yellow dye, while the darker inner bark will make a reddish dye.

The twigs can be bundled together to make a broom head as they are flexible and will not snap as they are swept over the floor.

Catkin covered spring twigs

placed in a vase make a decorative table display at a time of year when other hedgerow offerings are scarce.

Birch is considered by many cultures to be a purificatory or cleansing herb. The twigs are used to make whisks for dipping in water and striking yourself with during a Finnish sauna experience to enhance the cleansing process, whilst providing a pleasant aroma. The twigs are also used in exorcism style procedures where they are employed to gently strike either man or beast that has allegedly been possessed by a spirit.

Rope for binding can be made by choosing a long, thin branch and wrapping the thinnest end around your hand. Then just twist and continue to wrap it around. This process will break the wood fibres inside and leave you with a strong and flexible but simply made length of rope. Finer cordage can be made by stripping the fibres from the inner bark of either downy or silver birch and twisting.

Faggots can be used for the revetment and stabilisation of river banks.

A 'Y' shaped piece can be used to make the body of a catapult, every little boy's favourite. Birch wood can be carved into all number of children's toys, just use your imagination and you could end up with all the animals in a zoo!

Logs can be inoculated as a host for growing shiitake mushrooms.

Birch turns well for making decorative items and tool handles. It is favoured for these uses due to the strength of the wood and its beautiful grain.

Cradles for babies were traditionaly made from birch as in folklore it was a tree used for protection and so a cradle made from the wood would keep your newborn safe.

Birch wood is favoured in traditional ski making due to its flexibilty and is often still used as the wooden core of modern laminated skis. The qualities of the wood also make it good to use if building your own sledge/toboggan.

Birch wood can be milled and made into paper. Alternatively, fibre can be stripped from the inner bark to make paper. Harvest some branches of paper birch in spring or summer, remove the leaves and outer bark, then steam the branches. The fibres will peel off. Boil the fibres with lye or wood ash for a couple of hours before rinsing thoroughly, beating and spreading out to dry. The inner bark of both

downy and silver birch can be separated into thin layers and used as an oiled paper substitute without the need for any processing. Thin layers of inner bark have been used as manuscripts throughout history, the pressure sensitive surface retaining indentations made by a scribe with an instrument as crude as a sharpened stick. It can also be written on with ink, safe in the knowledge that even after the ink has faded, if the reader is determined, the words can still be read. Some First Nation peoples in northern Canada still use this part of the bark to make decorative items, indenting patterns with their teeth.

Sections of bark coiled into cylindrical shapes can be used as water resistant floats for fishing nets.

Baskets can be woven from thin strips of inner bark. Sheets of bark can also be folded and reinforced with small, bendy whips of willow or hazel and finally laced together with other naturally pliable materials such as willow root, making functional and decorative baskets.

Decorations can be woven from the bark such as hearts or stars to hang in the home or decorate a Christmas tree. Birch bark canoes, naturally waterproof and sealed with birch tar, make a light and durable craft. When the first

Europeans sought to exploit the great riches of the wild interior of Canada, copying the First Nation people's birch bark canoes was instrumental to their successful explorations and subsequent exploitation of that land. Imagine how satisfying it must be to navigate a watercourse in a canoe you have made yourself from locally available resources.

Oil distilled from the bark provides an effective insect repellant.

Birch tar can be used alone or mixed with beeswax as an adhesive to repair, for example, broken pots or fix arrowheads to the stems.

NOTES

10. Harley Refsal, *Celebrating Birch: The Lore, Art and Craft Of An Ancient Tree* (Fox Chapel Publishing Company Inc., 2007), 2.

11." *Edible Tree Saps"* Agroforestry Research Trust, Factsheet S07.

12. Harley Refsal, *Celebrating Birch: The Lore, Art and Craft Of An Ancient Tree* (Fox Chapel Publishing Company Inc., 2007), 5.

FLAX
(Linum usitatissimum)

FLAX ORIGINALLY CAME from india. Its latin name *linum usitatissimum* means 'most useful plant'. According to folklore flax is believed to help ward off poverty, a few seeds added to a wallet or purse being thought to attract money. An old remedy for dizziness is to run naked through a field of flax 3 times. Luckily this is to be done after sunset!

Strong fibres from the stem of flax have been widely used for thousands of years spun into yarn and woven into linen. Evidence of spinning flax fibres has been found in neolithic excavations from Syria, Mesopotamia (Iraq) and Persia (Iran) dating back to around 8000-6000 BC. Paintings detailing the spinning of flax yarn have even been found in ancient Egyptian tombs dating back to approximately 1900 BC, illustrating the importance of this fibre. The seed of flax, linseed, is also highly regarded, being the richest vegetable source of ALA (alpha linolenic acid), the plant based omega 3 fatty acid[13]. The seed contains 30-40% oil, consisting mainly of omegas 3 and 6. It also contains oleic acid (omega 9), the mono unsaturated fatty acids which make up between 60-80% of the fatty acids found in olive oil. As such it could be classified as a superfood that you can grow right in your own backyard!

Do not confuse this pretty and delicate looking plant with New Zealand flax though, which is in fact a phormium, an entirely different plant that also has multiple uses including medicine, weaving and basketry.

Varieties

Ornamental varieties have been developed but these have weaker fibre bundles, making them unsuitable for processing into linen.

Linum usitatissimum is a tall variety with few branches or flowers and good for fibre production.

Linum angustifolium is the wild form of flax and is a common weed throughout the Mediterranean that can also be found growing wild in Britain.

Growth Habits

Flax is an annual, although some varieties are biennial. It prefers loamy, well drained, humus rich soil in a sunny position. The small, delicate flowers of the flax plant are five petalled and are usually blue, although white ones are also found. The flowers sit upon tough, flexible stalks. It prefers a cool, moist climate, yet can tolerate a great range of temperatures, illustrated by the fact it can be found growing from Egypt, through much of Europe to China. It is quite a greedy feeder

and can deplete soils, so it's best grown in rotation, not returning to the same patch for 5 or 6 years. It grows well as a companion with both potatoes and carrots[14].

To produce the long, straight stems required for good quality fibre and linen production, sow at a spacing of 5cm. The densely packed seedlings will crowd each other, growing straight and tall without wasting energy on unwanted side branches. A spacing of 10cm between plants will encourage branching, the development of more flowers and hence greater seed production. Sow at a depth of 2cm in spring after the main risk of heavy frost has passed. Flax does not survive transplanting well so it is best sown where it can grow to maturity. For the most part flax is self-pollinating, although insects will provide some cross pollination. Each flower will develop into a spherical seed capsule approximately 1cm in diameter and containing 4-10 seeds, yielding between 1000 and 4000kg of seed per hectare.

Maintenance

Flax is a wild flower and so, on the whole, has maintained its inherent strength needing little attention. Apply a light mulch layer around the base to maintain moisture and organic matter content of the soil whilst reducing competition from weeds. Cutting off side branches on fibre crops will ensure good air circulation and reduce susceptibility to fungal infection, blight and rust.

HARVESTING, PROCESSING AND STORAGE

After around 3 months of growth flax should have reached a height of 90-120cm with the lower section of stem beginning to turn yellow. This is the best time to harvest for fibre, although the seeds will not have matured fully. Pull the entire plant up from the roots rather than cutting the stem as the fibres run from the root to the tip of the plant and maintain greater strength when left intact. Gather the stalks in bundles and hang to dry for a couple of weeks before further processing. The immature seeds can still be used from plants harvested at this point. Thresh by bashing the dried stems against a solid surface and the seeds will fall and can be collected. Alternatively, remove the seeds by passing the heads through a coarse comb.

If you are growing for seed only, leave the plants in the ground for a further month whilst the seeds ripen. Don't wait for the whole plant to die back but watch for the point when approximately 90% of the seed capsules are brown. Then either cut the stems and hang upside down to dry with newspaper beneath to catch the falling seed or store the seed capsules in a paper bag and wait for the seeds to be released. Ripe seeds may be stored whole in a cool dark place or pressed for oil (cold pressing is essential which means not above 34°C/93°F). To ensure maximum shelf life store the oil in dark glass and keep it refrigerated.

USES

FOOD

The seeds are an important source of omega 3 oils. Omega 3s are EFAs (essential fatty acids) and they cannot be manufactured within the body, so have to come from an external source. The seeds are low in carbohydrates and high in nutrients including magnesium, a mineral in which most western adults are deficient. Add them to salads, sprinkle over dishes before serving or add to smoothies either whole or as an oil. You can also make crackers from them by soaking the seed for a couple of hours, mixing it with herbs, garlic, chilli, tamari as your taste dictates then spreading thinly on a non stick sheet and dehydrating at a temperature of no more than 40°C (105°F) for several hours until crisp. Store in an air tight container. The seeds have a nutty smell and can be crushed in a coffee grinder to produce flax meal or flour. Once crushed the high oil content makes the seed meal go rapidly rancid, so only prepare a small amount at a time. If you do crush more than you intend to use, store them in an air tight container in the refrigerator. Flax seed flour added to baked goods such as cookies and muffins gives a rich, golden colour and added health benefits. Unripe seed capsules may be eaten raw straight from the plant.

The seed can be sprouted, although this is not as straightforward as it is with the majority of seed because once soaked flax becomes coated with a slimy film. To sprout them successfully you will need to use a sprout bag (see resources p185) as opposed to a tray or the usual sprouting device. Lay the sprout bag flat and spread a layer of seed over it, then spray with water using a plant mister. Do not let the seeds dry out. They will require regular misting over for the first couple of days then reduce it to just twice daily. They will take up to two weeks to be ready to eat and can then be stored for a few days in the fridge until eaten. Allow the length of the shoot to reach at least the length of the seed before eating or the taste will be very bitter.

Flax oil has a very short shelf life so if you are pressing yourself only do a small amount at a time. Store in a dark container, preferably

glass, and keep refrigerated. Always smell before use to check for rancidity. Never heat flaxseed oil or cook with it and it should only be used cold. If you are buying ready pressed oil from a shop make sure it is cold pressed, unrefined, unfiltered and refrigerated. Any processing of the oil will reduce its health giving qualities. Using the oil in foods is a great way to ingest healthy fats while stabilizing blood sugar and energy levels, giving the feeling of being full for longer. The oil can be added to salad dressings and smoothies or drizzled over soups just before serving. Adding flax oil to desserts will also make them feel more filling and satisfying so that you eat less. Make a dessert topping by mixing the oil ½ and ½ with either maple syrup or honey. It will cut down the sweetness but fill you more. You could mix whole seed with fresh fruit or yoghurt for a simple healthy option.

MEDICINE

Omega 3s are essential for the body's healthy function, a deficiency of which has been associated with more than 40 common diseases and conditions including fatigue, constipation, aching joints, arthritis, immune system dysfunction, hormonal imbalances, obesity, learning disabilities, osteoporosis, multiple sclerosis and stroke. Having the right balance of omega 3s (of which the alpha linolenic acid contained by flax is only one of 3) in your system will help guard against the onset of auto-immune conditions (where the body attacks its own cells e.g. rheumatoid arthritis), cardiovascular disease and cancer. Mood disorders including outbursts of violent behaviour can stem from a lack of omega 3s in the nerve cells of the brain. Consuming the seed or oil regularly can help moderate moods, lift depression and improve some cases of agoraphobia, schizophrenia, ADHD and bipolar disorder. Omega 3s also inhibit platelet aggregation and so protect against undesirable blood clots which can cause heart attack and stroke, whilst normalising blood pressure. Just one tablespoon of oil a day can help protect the body from the aforementioned conditions whilst improving the condition of skin, hair and nails.

Oil used as a dietary supplement will alleviate eczema, menstrual problems, rheumatoid arthritis and guard against the development of arteriosclerosis. Incorporating flax into the diet during pregnancy will aid in brain and visual function development in the growing foetus. Add 3 tablespoons of the oil to your diet daily throughout your pregnancy and whilst you are breast feeding. It is important to keep up your levels of

omega 3s whilst breastfeeding as they are crucial to your child's healthy development and you do not want to risk becoming depleted yourself as a deficiency can be a contributory factor to post natal depression.

When consumed whole or as meal you will have the added benefit of digesting the seed hulls. The hulls contain lignans which have antibacterial, antiviral and antioxidant properties. The antioxidant qualities help protect against free radical damage, implicated in disease development and premature ageing. In particular lignans have been shown to prevent the development of breast and colon cancers due to their ability to normalise hormone metabolism[15]. In addition lignans lower LDLs and raise HDLs which will help to protect the cardiovascular system against arteriosclerosis. Lignans also help to reduce the common symptoms related to PMS and menopause whilst regulating menstrual cycles. Flax is a great source of phytohormones which cause hormonal changes similar to those caused by the isoflavones found in soy products, making flax a good alternative to soy for treating menopausal symptoms. There is also evidence that consumption of flax will alleviate discomfort caused by poly-cystic ovary syndrome. Male reproductive health can also benefit from flax as the omega 3s will significantly enhance semen fertility.

Eating the seed provides mucilage which helps cleanse the intestinal tract, reducing the risk of colon cancer. Flax is a good source of fibre, essential for the efficient functioning of a healthy body. Crushed seed mixed with food and washed down with liquid acts as a bulk laxative for cases of chronic constipation and diverticulitis. Fibre in the diet also affects blood glucose levels helping the control and prevention of type II diabetes whilst lowering cholesterol and triglycerides, helping to prevent heart disease. A tablespoon of flaxseed provides 2-3g of fibre (the recommended daily allowance being 30g per day).

Flax is also anti-inflammatory, expectorant and its mucilaginous nature has a soothing effect on irritated tissues. Its consumption can help alleviate the symptoms of asthma. The soaked seeds can be consumed for the treatment of gastritis and pharyngitis and additionally they can be made into a poultice applied topically to relieve pain. A poultice of soaked seed mixed with white mustard can be placed on the chest for the relief of chest complaints. Infuse the seeds and mix with lemon and honey to relieve sore throats, coughs and chest conditions.
There are no reported cautions or contraindications for consuming flax oil or flax seed in medicinal doses.

CLOTHING

Just beneath the outer bark of the flax stem are bundles of shiny fibres and within each bundle there are between 15 and 40 individual strands of fibre. It is these fibres that are used to make linen. Flax has a long history of use as a fabric due to its strength and pleasing sheen. Linen is ideally suited to hot climates as it absorbs moisture and therefore sweat, allowing the skin to remain relatively dry whilst having a cool feel due to its high heat conductivity. As a downside linen lacks elasticity and creases easily but is tear resistant and stronger than cotton. Commercially linen has lost popularity over the last 100 years or so with the invention of modern fabrics, although being natural and sustainable it is set to make something of a comeback.

To make linen take the harvested stems that have been hanging to dry for the last couple of weeks. The organic material that surrounds the fibres now needs to be removed and there are several ways of achieving this. The first, known as 'dew-retting', allows dew to act on the woody matter and cellular tissue, rotting it away and leaving the long fibres intact. Simply spread the stems thinly on a patch of grass and leave for between 20-30 days. If this is done during a particularly dry period there will be insufficient dew to 'ret' the fibres and they will need to be lightly watered to allow the decomposition of the unwanted parts to be complete. It will take practice to get it just right so that the fibres themselves remain undamaged. This method produces a slightly darker end product than the second method which is known as 'water-retting'. Water-retting involves submerging the flax bundles in flowing water or dammed up pools for 10-14 days. This does cause a terrible smell and if you have access to a fresh water course, be careful not to let the debris wash downstream as although organic in origin, it's so concentrated that it is considered a pollutant.

The fibres then need to be completely dried before the flax straw is 'broken'. This can be achieved by smashing up and down the length of the straw with a mallet. Broken straw then needs to be removed before passing the fibres through a series of progressively smaller combs to remove any remaining remnants of straw. As the bundles are combed, short fibres known as 'tow' will fall to the floor, leaving 'line' or long fibres. Once collected in bundles tow is used to make coarser yarn while the line

produces a finer yarn.

Next the fibres need to be spun into yarn using a spinning wheel or by hand. All that is left to do at this point is to weave your yarn into fabric! This may sound like a labour intensive and laborious process but it was something our ancestors routinely did to clothe themselves. Tools for the process were often given as wedding gifts throughout Europe, showing how important and common this kind of processing was in each household. In fact, throughout Europe from the early middle ages until the end of the 1700s each house would grow sufficient flax for its own needs and rents were often paid with a bolt of linen cloth. Additionally, a chest full of linen was saved and given as a bride's dowry, a tradition continued by early settlers in North America.

FUEL

The stems can be burned and give off a similar heating value per ton as soft coal. It is cheaper than conventional fuels and carbon neutral, giving flax a great potential for generating energy in large scale burners as well as at home.

Seed cake, the fibrous by-product of cold pressing for oil, can be compressed into pellets for burning in pellet stoves or briquettes which can be burned as an alternative to wood or coal. Briquettes can burn for up to 3 times as long as wood and give off up to twice the amount of heat. They can be used in stoves, wood burners and open fires where they will produce less smoke than wood.

BUILDING AND HOUSING

The stalks can be baled tightly and used in straw bale construction, making well insulated, low impact and cost effective housing.

HOUSEHOLD

Flax (linseed) oil can be used as a protective treatment for floor boards and wooden furniture as on oxidation it provides a naturally hard wearing protective film. The oil can also be used in the manufacture of paints and varnishes.

Tablecloths, napkins, tea towels and sheets can all be made from linen.

GARDEN

Linen items that are worn through can be used as a slow rotting mulch around the garden.

MISCELLANEOUS

Seed residue (left after it has been pressed for oil extraction) is used to make

omega rich cattle feed or 'cattle cake'. This should only ever be given in small amounts and can also be fed to pigs.

The seed can be used in bird seed mixes to feed wild birds. It can also be fed to chickens, the high omega content improving the quality of their eggs.

Stem fibre can be made into paper.

Cloth woven from 'line' was used extensively in the past to make sail cloth for boats. This hard wearing canvas can also be made into awnings, horse coats and cloth bags. Linen canvas is also used by artists for painting; this use goes back to Egyptian times. The coarser material or 'tow' can be woven into sackcloth.

String and rope can be made from the fibre and if you have the patience you could go as far as to make a fishing net.

The oil can be burned in lamps to provide lighting while the yarn can be used for the wicks.

NOTES

13. Herb Joiner-Bey, *The Healing Power Of Flax* (Freedom Press, 2004), 8.

14. Ken Fern, *Plants For A Future; Edible & Useful Plants For A Healthier World* (Permanent Publications, 1997), 224.

15. Herb Joiner-Bey, *The Healing Power Of Flax* (Freedom Press, 2004), 10.

GARLIC
(Allium sativum)

GARLIC IS A member of the allium family, along with chives, shallots, leeks and onions. Throughout history garlic has been revered as an elixir of life, known to help strengthen the body and its internal organs, consequently helping ward off infection and disease. There are inscriptions in Egypt depicting garlic being fed to workers building the great pyramid to enhance their strength and stamina. In folklore garlic has always represented protection and has been carried by sailors, soldiers and even mountaineers for that very reason. Around the home it is said to protect against the intrusion of evil spirits and of course will keep you safe from bloodthirsty vampires!

Despite garlic's well known health benefits, master yoga practicioners will tend, for the most part, to avoid eating garlic as it is considered to be a *rajasic* food. Rajasic foods promote activity and hence a restless mind and so deter the yogis from their path of oneness and spiritual transcendence.

Recently after cutting back a Blackthorn hedge I was left with a large thorn under the skin on one of my fingers. I picked, sucked and chewed at it for days until it had become slightly infected, but luckily with one final squeeze the thorn popped out and I was left with a pussy wound on my finger. I suddenly remembered what to do and cut a slither from a bulb of garlic and wiped it back and forth over the wound. I did this only the once but within hours the infection had cleared up and I was just left with a small dry scab - that is the miracle of garlic!

VARIETIES

Allium sativum
There are many cultivars available and it is worth seeking out one that has been bred to grow in your climate. I find that Solent Wight does well here in Gloucestershire.

GROWTH HABITS

Garlic likes an open, sunny site with a light, free draining soil. It does not like acidic soils and will not grow if the acidity is of a greater level than pH 6.7. If this is the case just add some ground limestone or wood ash which will reduce the acidity. Plant in mid to late autumn or in early to mid spring. Spring plantings are best for heavy soils as winter rains can otherwise cause the bulb to rot in the ground.

Garlic must be one of the easiest plants to grow. Simply take a bulb and break it into cloves, ensuring that the papery covering of the individual cloves is not damaged. Push the clove root end downward into the soil to about the depth of your thumb (5cm) with a spacing of 7-10cm between cloves. It is best to get your bulbs from a specialist garlic producer (see resources) or garden supplier who will have varieties suitable for your conditions. You can try with supermarket garlic but the results are unlikely to be as good.

Although typically grown as an annual, garlic is in fact a perennial and can be left in the soil for several years. Leaving garlic to grow for more than one season will leave you with much smaller cloves, but many more of them when you do finally harvest.

MAINTENANCE

Although mainly trouble free with regards to pests and diseases it is worth rotating your garlic crop. Planting them in the same patch, or where other alliums have grown year after year, will increase their susceptibity to onion white rot. If you see any signs of this fungus you must destroy all affected plants and not grow any alliums on that patch for 15 years. Rust, appearing as small orange blisters on the leaves, may also affect garlic but is less serious and the chances of infection are reduced if you apply wood ash to the soil in early spring.

Garlic takes very little maintenance, just a little

weeding and watering during dry spells. It does not need feeding, although a little rock dust and/or potash will definately improve the size. It will grow best in soil that has been manured for the previous year's crop, not recently. Break off any flowers that start to form as these will take energy from the developing bulb.

Harvesting, Processing and Storage

At some point in mid to late summer the leaves will start to go brown and flop over. This is the best time to harvest. Lift the bulb and remove any attached clods of soil before leaving it to dry in a warm, well aerated place for a couple of weeks before storing. Once dry trim off the roots, then plait the leaves to make a traditional looking garlic string. This is not as simple as it looks so my prefered alternative is to clip off the leaves and tie the remaining stumpy tops at intervals along a piece of string. This is functional but in my opinion this still looks attractive hanging in the kitchen. If you have a large harvest they may be stored in a garage or shed, as long as they are protected from damp and frost.

USES

Food

Garlic is used widely, especially in Mediterranean cuisine. There are so many recipes which include garlic that I wont even try to represent them here as I'm sure you already have your favourites. I love roasting cloves to eat alongside a Sunday dinner and adding whole bulbs to a casserole or stew, then separating out the soft garlic puree amongst the assembled plates. Most of all I love using garlic raw, whether adding it to home made houmus or guacamole or simply slicing it thinly as part of a cracker topping.

It is not just the clove that can be eaten but also the green, fleshy stalks that are above ground and the flowers. The flowers always need to be removed if you are cultivating for the bulb, so this is a handy by-product that, like the leaves, can be sliced thinly and added to salads, or slipped into the blender when making pesto. Both the leaf and the flower have a milder flavour than the cloves themselves, perhaps making them easier to eat raw for those with a more delicate palate. Removing the leaves to eat is not a great idea as this is the powerhouse where the garlic absorbs the sun's energy and converts it to growth in the slowly maturing bulb, although harvesting the odd section wont hurt. If you are leaving your garlic to continue to grow for more than one season the leaves will pick up again later in the year and can be harvested for eating during the winter months.

Medicine

Garlic has a higher sulphur content than any other vegetable and this is one of its key attributes as a medicinal herb. It also has a high germanium content, germanium having cancer preventing properties and in addition stimulates the circulation of oxygen throughout the body which benefits all round levels of health. Garlic is a very powerful disinfectant capable of killing both typhoid bacteria and cholera causing bacteria. It has strong germicidal properties not found in other plants, and even diluted as much as 200 times allicin which is found in garlic will kill the typhoid bacteria[16]. In addition it is up to 15 times stronger than penicillin as an antibacterial agent.

Eaten regularly raw garlic is a fantastic medicine.Start with one clove a day, building up to three. Raw garlic acts as a preventative medicine and helps increase stamina as it cleanses and thereby improves the function and efficiency of the body's internal organs. It will boost your immune
80

system, help you fight colds, flu, viruses and sweat out a fever. It can ease and reduce the frequency of asthma and wheezing, help the respiratory system fight and recover from coughs, whooping cough, bronchitis, chest infections, sinusitis and clear out catarrh. It cleans the blood, protecting your body from toxins whilst imparting an improved feeling of vitality. It has an anti-obesity action, can help reduce cholesterol, lower high blood pressure and reduce arteriosclerosis. Eating garlic also warms the body and stimulates the liver, kidneys and blood circulation whilst improving the absorbtion of vitamins. It is a well celebrated remedy for heart complaints including angina and can reduce the risk of stroke, thrombosis and heart attack. It is of benefit when suffering from gastrointestinal problems including gastritis, gastric ulcer and even some cases of stomach cancer whilst reducing flatulance and incidences of indigestion. Eating a small piece of garlic before bed will ease constipation. In addition garlic improves the balance of bacteria in the gut so always eat plenty after a course of antibiotics. It can help clear up a Candida albicans overgrowth and reduce any yeast infections caused by the Candida. Garlic has pain killing properties and can ease menstrual cramps, arthritis, rheumatism, neuralgia and sciatica. Eating it regularly will help acne outbreaks clear up and will deter mosquito bites. Don't forget to chew a sprig of parsley after eating garlic to banish the strong odour.

Crush a few cloves, mix with a jar of honey and use two teaspoons daily either added to hot water or eaten directly from the spoon to treat colds, coughs, tonsilitis and soothe a sore throat. The sweetness disguises the taste, making it palatable to children.

Gargling with diluted garlic juice will soothe and heal tonsillitis and sore throats. If you do not have a juicer grate raw garlic into water, leave to infuse for 30 minutes, strain and gargle with the mixture for the same effect.

Garlic can stimulate the bowels, kill intestinal parasites and help them pass from the body. Juice a clove with a small piece of ginger and dilute in a ratio of 1:5 with water. Drink this and follow it with 2 glasses of water. It is important to do this in the morning on an empty stomach and then for the rest of the day eat only plain steamed rice. During the following days add raw garlic to your diet until all symptoms have passed and the worms have been excreted. This may seem drastic but the pharmaceutical drugs used for this purpose are often particularly toxic with some alarming potential side effects.

Slice a clove of raw garlic and rub it on insect bites to reduce the soreness and on minor cuts, grazes and wounds for its antibacterial properties. Also rub it over abscesses on the gums and under the teeth. When applied topically in this way garlic will also help clear athlete's foot, thread worm, ring worm and warts.

Infuse in oil and rub on cold feet to encourage circulation. Apply the oil topically to relieve sprains, aches, muscle pain, arthritis and neuralgia. For earache and ear infections warm a little on a spoon and dribble into the ear, plugging with cotton wool for an hour by which time the oil will have been absorbed.

Use with caution if on blood thinning medication and do not consume in medicinal doses if breastfeeding as it may cause colic in your infant.

FUEL

Add the stalks to other dry garden waste and make cellulosic ethanol with which you can run a petrol engine (see p172).

GARDEN

Garlic is a known deterrent for a whole host of garden pests including ants, aphids, earwigs, slugs, snails, and whitefly. Take a few cloves, mash or juice them, mix with 500ml of plain or soapy water and leave to infuse for at least an hour. Use this first thing in the morning or at dusk and spray both the tops and the underside of leaves on plants you would like to protect. Never spray in the middle of the day as this may damage the foliage, especially if the sun is strong. The mixture will store in the fridge for a week.

Garlic is well revered in the garden as a companion plant. It grows well with lettuce from which it deters aphids, carrots from which it deters carrot root fly and beetroot and cabbage where again it deters many pests and actually enhances their flavour. It is also a well known companion for roses, apples and peaches. It is not a garden panacea however and should be grown separately from beans, pulses, peas and potatoes. Companion planting is especially relevant if you are growing organically as it is a way of using the properties of certain plants to the benefit of others growing in their vicinty, helping to reduce pest damage.

MISCELLANEOUS

Garlic is an aphrodisiac, most probably due to the flush of blood and vigour throughout the body. The smell on your breath may however put off amorous admirers unless you eat the garlic together. If that's

not the case then chewing on a sprig of parsley is advisable as this will neutralise the smell.

A simple glue can be made by crushing a clove and rubbing it on the material you want to stick. Simply place the other piece on top. This works well for paper and can be used to stick pieces of glass and even broken china together.

Take a slice of raw garlic and rub it over acne before bed every night. This is very effective but be sure to wash thoroughly before leaving the house to remove the odour. Alternatively, make an antibacterial skin wash by infusing a couple of crushed garlic cloves in hot water. Allow the water to cool to a pleasant temperature then apply to the face with a clean wash cloth. This is more gentle than rubbing the cloves directly onto your face. As with all skin care, patch test on the inside of your arm first to check you are not sensitive to using garlic topically.

Crush a clove or two of garlic and leave for several hours in a jug of water to infuse. Strain to remove the garlic pieces and use to rinse your hair and massage into your scalp. This will stimulate hair growth and prevent dandruff. As an alternative simply rub fresh garlic into your scalp which will have a stronger action. A short time after either treatment it is advisable to wash your hair thoroughly with mild shampoo to rid it of the smell.

To make a mosquito repellent crush or grate a couple of cloves and mix with water or dilute fresh garlic juice 1:10 with water and put it in a spray bottle. If you are planning on being alone or have game friends or family then spray yourself liberally at dusk when those little critters start bugging you. If your skin experiences any reaction to this mixture I suggest you wash it off immediately as garlic is very strong and can be a skin irritant. If the irritation is coming from small cuts or grazes you are probably doing yourself a favour and the spray is acting as a disinfectant, killing bacteria around the wound site - a double bonus! If you do not want the spray on your skin you can spray your clothes or mosquito net with it, although you will still of course smell!

Feeding small amounts of garlic to your pets along with their regular food at meal times will help to repel ticks, fleas and parasites. Just try a tiny pea sized piece every now and then to keep them clear, or daily if they are currently suffering an infestation. Cease daily usage once they are clear. Garlic is also often used to keep horses in prime condition with a healthy, glossy coat. They will need a higher dose as their bodies

are much larger but there has been evidence suggesting that garlic in the diet of both horses and dogs can cause anaemia so it is important to only give it when you think they will benefit and not constantly. Discontinue the use of garlic with your animals if you think they are suffering any adverse effects.

Adding garlic to the diet of chickens will help them to continue laying eggs during very cold or very hot spells. Simply grate a pea sized piece of garlic in their water daily. This quantity is for 5-10 chickens so adjust it accordingly for the size of your flock.

Coating marshmallows with garlic powder works as fishing bait, attracting bass and trout amongst others. To make your own garlic powder either slice several cloves finely and place in a dehydrator or at a low temperature in the oven until crisp. Crush finely using a pestle and mortar and roll the marsmallows in the powder. Keep any that you don't immediately use in an airtight container otherwise the powder will absorb moisture and become sticky.

NOTES

16. Yoshio Kato, *Garlic: The Unkown Miracle Worker* (Oyama Garlic Laboratory, 1973), 174.

HAZEL
(Corylus avellana)

KNOWN AS THE *tree of immortal wisdom*, hazel is a deciduous broadleaf native to the UK. In folklore the nuts of the hazel pass on divine wisdom and excellent intuition. The fact that they are also tasty makes them more than worthy of the occassional munch. To the Celts water was seen as the entrance to the 'Otherworld' and offerings could be made to the Gods by dropping hazelnuts into lakes and wells. In fact it has many associations with faerie lore and is said to allow entrance into such realms so it's not surprising that the wood has been favoured for making staffs, both for druidic ritual use and for pilgrims.

Hazel is often planted in hedgerows and enjoys a similar microclimate to apples, so if you have productive apple trees then hazel is more than likely to also be productive. Hazel is often coppiced and provides a hardwood that is pale brown in colour.

VARIETIES

American hazel/filbert *(Corylus americana)* grows to a height of 2.7m with small nuts growing in clusters of between 2 and 4.

Beaked hazelnut *(Corylus cornuta)* grows to a height of 1.8m.

European hazel/filbert *(Corylus avellana)* grows to a height of 4.5m. The cultivar Hall's

Giant has exceptional yields, producing over 8kg per tree in trials[17].

Cobnut is another common name for cultivated varieties and Cosford Cob, Kentish Cob and Webb's Prize Cobnuts all produce large sized nuts.

Growth Habits

Hazel prefers moist, well drained calcareous soils and will not survive if the soil is really dry. Hazel thrives in soils with a pH ranging from 5.5 to 7.5, prefering fertile soil. It is shade tolerant but will not bear a large quantity of nuts under a very heavy, closed canopy, for example in the midst of an oak wood or if the soil is exceptionally fertile. It is tolerant of frost and wind making it a useful hedging tree if you live in a cold or exposed area. Despite its more hardy properties you will get a greater yield of nuts if your tree receives full sun and is protected from strong winds by surrounding trees and shrubs. It is preferable to have other hazels nearby to facilitate pollination and having a minimum of three different varieties would be the optimum, although the presence of wild hazels in the vicinity would also suffice.

To grow a new hazel take a fresh nut and plant it in a pot with compost. Protect it from squirrels and mice until it has germinated. Keep in a pot for the first couple of years before planting out. Hazel can also be propagated by layering which involves taking a still attached stem in late winter, scraping the bark from the underside and pegging it to the ground. In a couple of years roots will have developed and it can be cut from the mother tree.

Young trees take between 5-7 years before producing nuts and a full 15 years before you get maximum productivity which can be as high as 11kg per tree[18]. Like many fruit trees, good yields of hazel nuts tend to be biennial. The life span of hazel is only 60-80 years, although this can be lengthened significantly if it is coppiced. A 6-10 year rotation can provide wood for hurdles, bean poles and thatching spars. A one hectare area dedicated to hazel coppice that is 8 or 9 years old can produce 25,000-30,000 rods with lengths of around 3-4.5m[19]. Small diameter sticks and poles from hazel can be twisted and bent without breaking.

Maintenance

Nuts may require protection due to a proliferation of grey squirrels and the lack of a suitable predator, a perfect example of the consequences of a habitat (or planet) out of balance. The squirrel problems seem to be worse if your hazel is close to a mature tree that is providing shelter and potentially a home for them. If you are growing a large number of hazel then there will be plenty for both yourself and the squirrels.

A little pruning to keep your trees uncongested will aid you when it comes to harvesting the nuts.

HARVESTING, PROCESSING AND STORAGE

Gather leaves for eating and medicinal uses in spring when they are young and fresh. Dry for times when there are no fresh leaves available by separating and placing them in a single layer on newspaper in a warm spot but out of direct sunlight. Once dry they can be stored in an airtight container until needed.

Nuts are produced every year and collected in the autumn as the leaves change colour. Once gathered store your nuts in a cool, dry place for around six weeks before shelling. This gives time for their flavour to enrich as they dry. You can store the unshelled nuts for years in dry salt or sand. The shells are very hard, making a nut cracker an essential tool.

USES

FOOD

Wild hazels have a richer flavour than the larger cobnuts. The nuts are very nutritious, being rich in phosphorus, potassium, magnesium, copper, zinc and protein. They can be eaten as they come or added to all kinds of recipes, from my mum's delicious hazelnut roulade to nut burgers. Flour made from the nuts is used in many traditional German recipes.

The nuts can be cold pressed to produce a golden, nutritious oil. Consuming this oil will nourish the skin and hair, giving it a healthy and glossy appearance. You can cook with this oil but I prefer not to, choosing to simply use it cold in salad dressings, and in this way preserving the delicious, nutty flavour. Once pressed store in a cool, dark place, preferably in a dark glass container. It will remain good for 3-4 years.

Truffles are sometimes found growing amongst hazel roots, although you may need a well trained porcine friend to help you find them!

MEDICINE

Constituents within the leaves support collagen in the body's connective tissues and lungs. The leaves are also astringent, antiparasitic and support the healing of wounds. They can be eaten fresh or more popularly made into an infusion and drunk up to 3 times daily. Drunk regularly over time the infusion will help improve the appearance of varicose veins. The infusion will also treat diarrhoea, coughs and heal bruising. Make a litre or two of leaf infusion, pour into a bowl and allow to cool so it is comfortable to the touch. Soak hands and/or feet in the infusion to improve circulation and bring relief from chillblains. Eating a few nuts regularly will help improve the function of your immune system due to their high zinc content.

There are no reported cautions or contraindications for using hazel leaf medicinally.

Fuel

Hazel wood takes approximately 18 months to season fully. Make sure it has been well seasoned and it will make a good quality fuel wood which burns quite fast but does not spit. It can also be made into good quality charcoal.

Bundles of brushwood trimmings make good kindling.

Building and Housing

Staples or broches made from thin sections of hazel are used to hold thatch in place on roofs and pegs and spars used in thatching can be made from hazel rods. To make spars of the appropriate straightness and thickness they need to be in an 8 year coppice cycle. Thin strips (laths) can be

woven into a lattice or nailed in rows to a framing support which can then be used as a substructure for plaster work or roofing where slates, shingles or tiles can be laid.

Household

The wood can be used for making rustic furniture.

The oil can be used as a wood polish.

Garden

Pea sticks, bean poles, hurdles and fencing can all be made from thinnings.

The long poles used to bind the tops of stakes along lain hedges, known as hedging etherings, can be made from hazel. Hazel can also provide wood for the stakes themselves.

Collect the fallen leaves in autumn and store in black bags, moistening them a little with some water. After two years they will have produced a rich and fertile leaf mould that you can spread over your beds.

Hazel can be used as a hedgerow plant and makes an excellent windbreak, either mixed with other species or alone with a spacing of at least 3 or 4 paces between plantings. It plays host to a wide range of fauna making it an important part of the local ecosystem.

MISCELLANEOUS

Smaller cuttings can be woven into baskets.

Hazel is the traditional wood for making dowsing rods, utilised when searching for underground water sources.

The wood can be fashioned into walking sticks and made into toys or pegs for holding guy ropes.

The foliage can be used as cattle fodder.

Apply the nut oil directly to the skin and hair as an astringent, nourishing and moisturising beauty treatment that will impart a delicate nutty aroma. Hazelnut is a good oil to use on mature, sensitive and even baby skin. The oil will moisturise, soften and protect skin whilst stimulating circulation and is quickly and easily absorbed by the skin, leaving no greasy residue. The astringent action of the oil helps balance oily and combination skins. If you have dry or irritated skin combine with another oil before application to counterbalance the astringency. It acts as a natural sun filter and tones and firms skin whilst encouraging cell regeneration, making it ideal for use on more mature skin or where there are thread veins[20].

Fresh nuts can be crushed and massaged into the hair as a deep conditioning treatment believed to promote hair growth.

A strong leaf infusion can be dabbed on problem and oily skin with cotton wool. Its natural astringent properties will help dry up excess oils and close open pores.

NOTES

17. Martin Crawford "A.R.T. 2006 Trial Ground Report" Agroforestry News Volume 15, Number 2, February 2007, 7.

18. Patrick Whitefield, The Earth Care Manual (Permanent Publications, 2004), 222.

19. Elizabeth Agate, Woodlands: A Practical Handbook (BTCV Publications, 1980), 97.

20. Kolbjørn Borseth, The Aromantic Guide to Unlocking the Powerful Health & Rejuvenation Benefits of Vegetable Oils (Aromantic Ltd., 2008), 90.

HEMP
(Cannabis sativa)

HEMP IS NATIVE To central Asia and evidence of its cultivation has been found in China dating back to between 8000 and 6000BC, placing it alongside flax as one of the first plants humankind cultivated for fibre. Hemp symbolizes purity and fertility to followers of Shinto, the indigenous religion of Japan. It's a stalky crop grown both for its edible seed and strong fibres, whose use can be traced through almost all cultures. Before I continue to list the virtues of this most wonderful and versatile plant there is a need to make the distinction between it and marijuana. Marijuana, a member of the same species, is a more bushy plant that is well known for its mind altering capabilities and the active ingredient that gets you 'high' is THC (tetrahydrocannabinol). Hemp contains a trace amount of THC but it would be impossible to get high from its use. Marijuana has a much higher THC content contained in the resin which literally oozes out of the plant, forming sparkling crystals on the flower buds. You will not find such sticky crystal covered buds on a hemp plant. THC is a mildly analgesic substance used to treat pain and aid relaxation. It has been used medicinally across the globe for millennia and is currently used by aids and cancer sufferers, amongst others. Medical marijuana was legalized in Arizona and California in 1996 as its medicinal benefits were officially recognized. This plant profile is however dedicated specifically to low THC content hemp.

Historically hemp has played

a valuable role. Not only was it the most important crop for Britain's economy during the 1700s but across the ocean in 1640 it was declared by the governor of Connecticut that every resident of the colony must grow the plant. In fact the first two drafts of the US Declaration of Independence were written on hemp paper. Marijuana's cultivation was prohibited in the USA in 1937, and because of the apparent confusion between hemp and marijuana there is currently a large amount of prejudice against hemp, especially at governmental level, the USA being the worst offender. If this legislation had never been made then the use of hemp paper and plastics might have been much more widespread than paper derived from wood (ancient forests) and plastics from oil (ancient sunlight). What a different world we could have been living in! There would perhaps be less pollution, less dependence on fossil derived oil, less deforestation, but it doesn't help to think of what could have been. What is important is to act on what can be done. The only way to override the misplaced prejudice against hemp and hemp products is with education. Hemp does not equal marijuana. In many countries that were not influenced by American legislation hemp has continued to be an important crop. In France, for example, hemp has been cultivated uninterrupted

for over 600 years. The UK legislated against hemp production in 1971 but subsequently lifted its ban in 1993. That said you still need a Home Office license to legally grow hemp in the UK and only cultivars with a THC content of less than 0.2% may be grown within the EU. It is advisable to check the legalities of growing hemp in your locale before launching headlong into home production.

Hemp has an estimated 25,000 uses in everything from dynamite to cellophane. It can be grown and processed with little energy and without the need for toxic chemicals. It has been said that virtually everything currently made from trees or petroleum could instead be made from hemp. Consider that up to 50% of oil currently drilled from the earth is made into plastic, replace that with hemp plastic, especially in these environmentally conscious times, and suddenly growing hemp seems all the more relevant.

VARIETIES

Cannabis sativa
NB subspecies *indica* yields the narcotic variety marijuana.

GROWTH HABITS

Hemp is an annual plant that grows as a weed, especially in nitrogen rich soil and can reach a height of between 1.8m and almost 5m. It will grow in a wide range of climates, is highly resistant to disease and tolerant of insect attack whilst its rapid growth out competes weeds thus negating any worries about pesticide or herbicide use. On an industrial scale this is great news for the soil and local ecology. Hemp prefers a position in full sun with well drained soil that has a fine tilth and a good organic matter content. It will not flourish on waterlogged, light or poor soils lacking in organic matter. Despite hemp's preferences it can survive on heavily degraded and even slightly saline soils.

Some countries steam sterilize the seed to prevent germination, so be careful to make sure any seed you buy is live seed. When grown for fibre, hemp is planted densely at around 300-500 plants per square metre which discourages the growth of side branches and causes the hemp to grow tall and straight. Plant at a much lower density if growing primarily for the seed as this will encourage the growth of side shoots where flowers and seeds will then develop. Plant in late April or early May when the soil reaches a temperature of around 8-10°C (45°F). It can take a light frost but protect young shoots if heavy frost is predicted. Water well during the first month as this will help the plant establish and its roots develop, giving it the ability to cope with less water later in the growing season. Hemp does not exhaust the soil and can be grown in the same spot year after year, although it is always best to grow it in rotation. It has been reported to grow better following a nitrogen fixing plant such as beans or alfalfa.

Hemp is dioecious, meaning that it has separate male and female plants. Some varieties of industrial hemp have been bred to be monoecious, having both male and female flowers on each plant. Hemp will flower and then start producing fruit in late summer as the nights lengthen. Hemp seed is not actually true seed but rather an achene, which is a fruit containing a seed in a case. Males tend to start flowering a couple of weeks before the females and being wind pollinated it is necessary to have both to ensure pollination and production of seed. The females can be identified by the wispy white pistils that emerge from the calyxes of immature flowers. Only the females will produce seed. Once pollinated it will take a further 3-6 weeks for the seeds to mature.

MAINTENANCE

Hemp is pretty low maintenance. Just apply a phosphorus rich feed regularly once flowering begins.

HARVESTING, PROCESSING AND STORAGE

Hemp is harvested for its fibres before flowering. It will reach its full height approximately 3 months after sowing. As with other plants grown for their fibre it is best to take the whole plant from the ground so you do not damage the integrity of the fibres. Average fibre yields are around 7.5 t/ha in the UK. Processing of the stalks will differ depending on the intended use of the fibre. If making fibreboard, for example, the stalks can be used while green and chopped as needed. Bast fibre and hurds are obtained by removing outer layers of the stalk, and long fibres and tow are extracted by retting the stems. Leave the stems to dry for around 4 days after harvesting before dew retting for 2-3 weeks (for details see flax p74). Leave the stalks to ret in the field in which they grew as this will allow nutrients to leach back into the soil. Remove any leaves here as they will also rot away and reincorporate up to 50% of the nitrogen used in growth back into the earth. Turn the stalks halfway through the process to ensure even retting.

When harvesting the seed on a small scale you can hang the seed heads upside down and catch the falling seed on newspaper, or rub the dried flower heads to loosen the seed. Yields of around 1.25 t/ha can be expected in UK conditions. Seed will need to be stored in a dark, cool place, preferably in the fridge as the high oil content means they will quickly go rancid. I never have room in my fridge and find that if stored in an air tight container in a cool dry place they are still good to eat after a year.

USES

FOOD

Cold pressing hemp seed results in a thin oil which ranges in colour from deep green to a golden yellow, or liquid sunshine as I like to call it. The oil is delicious. I often add a dash to smoothies, salad dressings or use it on its own as a dip for fresh bread or as a topping on freshly made soup or pasta. It has a 3:1 balance between the essential fatty acids (EFAs) linoleic and alpha linolenic (omegas 3 and 6), which is claimed to be the optimal balance for human nutrition. It is worth noting that this balance between the EFAs is unique to hemp within the plant world. It also contains phosphorus, potassium, magnesium, sulphur, calcium and vitamin A alongside a small amount of iron and zinc. It has a naturally high content of polyunsaturated fatty acids so you should not cook with the oil and must use it within

6 months or it will go rancid. Always store it in a dark glass bottle in the fridge.

Hemp seed additionally supplies all eight of the essential amino acids. These are the amino acids that the body cannot produce by itself and so must be obtained from food. The EFAs and essential amino acids found in hemp help the body maintain strong, elastic, healthy tissues. A diet high in these nutrients will give you a vibrant appearance, especially benefiting your skin, hair, nails and eyes. So if you don't use the oil at least add some seed regularly to your diet. Just one handful of hemp seed a day equates to roughly 25% of the recommended intake of protein for adults. You can eat handfuls of seed as they come for a snack or add them as a crunchy topping to soups and salads. You can make hemp seed butter which is delicious and much more nutritious than peanut butter. Use ground or whole seed in all kinds of home made goodies like hemp seed burgers, cookies and cakes. Try mashing up fresh seed with a little garlic, chilli, sea salt and lime juice for a lively hemp seed chutney.

Hemp seed milk is easier for the body to digest than cow's milk. Simply take a handful of hemp seeds and soak them for 8 hours, blend them well with a pint of water then drain through a sieve to remove all the bits. Drink fresh or blend with fruits for a non-dairy milk shake. The waste bits that you sieve off can either be composted or made into delicious, raw and nutritious crackers. Just mix the bits with a cup of flax seed that have been soaking in water for an hour or two, spread thinly on a baking sheet then dehydrate (either in a dehydrator or in an oven at a temperature of no more than 40°C(105°F)) for a few hours until crisp.

Hemp seed can be sprouted and once the little tails appear can be added to salads or used in place of non sprouted seed in recipes. Grown on a little longer you can collect the leaf and eat it fresh in salads, juice it or dry and powder it. Add the powder to smoothies or the fresh juice to other fruit juices and enjoy it for its anti-aging and other health giving properties.

Hemp seed flour can be made by milling and sifting the seed cake (what's left after cold pressing it for oil). High in protein and gluten free, this flour can be used in baking but will not rise, so combine it with other flours unless making flat breads or crackers. Hemp is a relative of hops and the seed cake can be brewed into beer which will maintain its head for longer than beer brewed from the whole seed. There are many commercial hemp beers available across the world.

Again, be aware of steam sterilized seed if you don't have the space to grow hemp and are just buying in seed to eat. Once sterilized the seed will go rancid more quickly, will not sprout and will have reduced nutritional qualities. Always look for live seed or speak to the supplier to check that your seed has not been sterilized.

Medicine

The oldest reference to hemp as a medicine comes from China where for over 3000 years it has been considered one of the 'superior elixirs of immortality'. The Indian Pharmacopoeia of 1868 lists it as a remedy for tetanus, hydrophobia, delirium tremens, infantile convulsions, asthma, hay fever and protracted labour. In Japan hemp is known as a time proven remedy for constipation, asthma and skin problems.

Consuming 1-3 tablespoons of the oil daily has a wide array of medicinal benefits. The EFA content will help lower blood pressure by relaxing blood vessel walls, reducing the stickiness of platelets and thinning the blood. It will also reduce cholesterol. All these effects make it a useful part of a treatment regime for, or preventative medicine against angina, arteriosclerosis, high blood pressure, varicose veins, thrombosis, cardiac arrhythmia
94

and Raynaud's disease. The prostaglandins produced in your body as a result of ingesting hemp seed oil have a powerful anti-inflammatory effect and directly suppress allergic reactions. So again it can be used as a preventative medicine and as part of the treatment for eczema, dermatitis, psoriasis, hives, hay fever, asthma, osteo and rheumatoid arthritis and will even help with both Crohn's disease and ulcerative colitis. The EFAs also help to balance hormones, reducing menstrual pains, breast tenderness and PMS. Consuming 3 tablespoons a day will benefit your skin condition and tone. One friend ate 3 tablespoons a day throughout her pregnancy and avoided getting any stretch marks. It is a great idea to consume it during pregnancy as it will benefit your babies developing brain and central nervous system.

Use the oil when making herbal salves as it will enhance the healing action of the herbs, especially when used on irritated skin, insect bites, minor cuts and scrapes.

Eating the seeds regularly will help retain strength and fertility whilst easing digestive and urinary complaints. In addition regular consumption of hemp's high level of nutrients will help build a strong immune system, lower cholesterol and improve brain function whilst maintaining both nerve and joint health. Crushing the seeds into a paste and applying it directly to the skin will reduce inflammation and soothe abscesses, boils and pimples.

There are no reported cautions or contraindications for using hemp medicinally.

CLOTHING

Long fibres found in the stems are used for making fabric and have 3 times the tensile strength of cotton. They are also hollow which means they allow the passage of air more easily than many fabrics. The fibres are coarser than those of flax yet you can still weave the wonderful, soft, hard wearing fibres into all manner of clothing from fine weave undergarments and t-shirts, to more chunky weave scarves, hats and jackets. Lengths of hemp yarn can also be knitted into garments of your own design.

FUEL

The short fibres (hurds) can be burned to produce heat or processed into biomethanol (see p173) and used as a fuel in engines. If growing for the seed you could use the stalks as a byproduct to make bioethanol. Methanol or ethanol made from hemp has the additional benefit of being carbon neutral as it only puts back into the atmosphere

the same amount of CO_2 on burning as the hemp absorbed whilst growing. Oil obtained from the seed can also be used as a fuel and added to biodiesel blends.

BUILDING AND HOUSING

Hurds blended with lime make strong, lightweight blocks that can be used in place of concrete or breeze blocks in construction. The blocks are stronger and significantly lighter than concrete with excellent resistance to insect damage and mold. In addition they are naturally fire retardant and allow moisture vapour to pass through which helps protect timbers from decay. In addition hemp fibre walls have excellent insulating properties and a room made with walls 300mm thick would need virtually no heating to maintain a comfortable temperature inside. Hurds can also be combined with lime to be used in place of traditional plaster on both internal and external surfaces, including ceilings.

Hurds can be used as insulation, for example between walls. They will need treatment with a fire retardant to be safe but even after this treatment would cause less skin and lung irritation than using fibreglass insulation.

Chipped stalks can be used instead of woodchip in fibreboard and make a much stronger finished product. Hemp's bast fibres also make a strong, insect resistant and relatively fireproof fibreboard that could replace the woodchip and resin composite board often used in paneling and furniture making.

The stalks can be tightly baled and used as the straw in straw bale construction. The bales are placed together like bricks, providing great insulation and low impact, cost effective buildings.

HOUSEHOLD

The oil can be used in paints and varnishes.

Hemp fibres can be blended with wool and made into high quality, durable and soft to touch carpets.

GARDEN

Densely planted patches of hemp can help condition your soil. The deep tap roots help to aerate and break up compacted soils, whilst leaves that drop off during the growth cycle add a naturally nitrogen rich mulch to the top layer, increasing the soil's humus content and fertility.

Any hemp fabric that has come to the end of its useful life can be recycled into the environment in the form of a biodegradable mulch. The fabric will slowly rot and become part of the soil but

in the mean time will protect the soil from the elements and keep it weed free. It is especially useful as a mulch around young trees or other plants that need to have competition from weeds and grass around their base kept to a minimum.

Hemp grown for fibre can help improve the condition of land previously polluted with industrial heavy metals. Toxic waste is drawn up through hemp's roots and stored in the stem which, providing they are not subsequently combusted, can be put to use safely elsewhere, thus cleaning the soil[21].

Bast fibres can be processed and made into horticultural matting.

MISCELLANEOUS

Long line or long fibre is the longest length fibre that you get from hemp. They come from the outer part of the stalk and make up around 30% of the total fibres. They are stronger than cotton and have additional anti-mildew and antimicrobial properties that make these fibres ideal for use in awnings, tarpaulins, sails and carpets. The fibres can be made into rope and cordage. Hemp rope is believed to have been used during the building of the great pyramids in Egypt due to its superior strength. Ropes dating back 4000 years have been found in Thebes in Egypt. You can also make sturdy items like tents, bags, curtains, bedding, shoe uppers and upholstery from hemp fabric. The roots of the word canvas (the common name for this tough fabric) come from the word cannabis.

An acre of hemp yields as much as four times the amount of fibre as an acre of trees. Paper can be made from the fibre, making hemp a much more efficient raw material for paper making. In addition it grows more quickly than trees, further enhancing its credentials in this regard as the resource will renew at a greater speed. Hemp paper is naturally pliable, partially water resistant and is stronger than wood pulp paper. Some pieces of hemp paper have been dated back to 2000 years, proving its longevity. It is best to use tow (medium fibre) for paper making as it has low lignin levels. Converting hemp fibre to paper requires less chemical treatment and less energy input than is needed to break down tree fibres, making it more energy efficient and less polluting. In addition the inherent anti-mildew and antimicrobial properties make tow a good choice for making personal hygiene products such as nappies and sanitary towels[22].

Short core fibre also known as *hurds* or *shivs* can hold up to twice as much moisture as straw or wood shavings, making it a good choice for use as animal bedding for horses and domestic pets such as rabbits, hamsters and guinea pigs. Its high absorbency means it is also useful as cat litter. Alternatively, you can use these fibres to stuff a mattress for use by humans or as a packaging material.

The oil can be used externally on all skin types. It contains gamma linolenic acid (GLA) and so can be used on the skin like other GLA oils such as evening primrose and borage. The body will convert the GLA to prostaglandins, deficiencies of which contribute to dry skin which lacks firmness and elasticity with visible wrinkles. Such deficient skin will age more quickly and be more sensitive to sun while damaged skin will take longer to heal. Applying the oil to skin will help soften and improve moisture retention, guarding against dry skin. It is absorbed quickly and does not leave a greasy residue. You can use it neat on the face but as it is absorbed rapidly it's best to combine it with a longer oil such as sunflower if you are massaging over larger areas. It is ideal to use on sensitive skin that is affected by acne, eczema and psoriasis. Try combining it with avocado or apricot kernel oil for a thick and nourishing treatment.

Hemp oil can be used to

deeply condition the hair and bring relief from a dry, itchy scalp. It can also be used as an ingredient in soaps, shampoos, conditioners, lip salves, lotions and moisturisers.

After the oil has been pressed out from the seed the remains can be compressed into seed-cake. The protein content of seed-cake remains high at around 25% making it an excellent foodstuff for domestic pets, cows, horses and even chickens.

If you use lanterns for light use hemp oil as it burns cleaner and brighter than using kerosene or petroleum oil. Candles can be made from hemp oil for which you can even use a hemp wick.

Feed any excess seed to the birds. The nutritional qualities give improved condition to birds that eat it.

Hemp twine makes a superior washing line as it is naturally mold and mildew resistant and will last longer than most other ropes when left for extended periods exposed to the elements.

Perhaps on a more industrial scale but also worth noting is that the hurds are also the raw ingredient for hemp plastic which can of course be formed into all number of items from shower curtains to moulded chairs if you have

the right equipment. It can be processed and used as a substitute for fibreglass in boats, cars, surfboards and skateboards, to name but a few possibilities. A snowboard has even been created with a wood core wrapped in hemp. The oil blends well with other substances and so can be used as an ingredient in lubricants, printing inks and solvents. Hemp is being used in the automotive industry in a range of parts including airbags, gaskets, upholstery, panels and floor mats. In fact Henry Ford used hemp in the panels of some of his early cars. Anything made from the hydrocarbons in oil can be made from the carbohydrates in hemp (or other plants for that matter).

NOTES

21. John W. Roulac, *Hemp Horizons: The Comeback of the World's Most Promising Plant* (Chelsea Green Publishing Company, 1997), 131.

22. Ibid., 14.

HOPS
(Humulus lupus)

HOPS ARE A member of the cannabaceae family which also includes hemp. Hops are associated with good luck and as such are often used at weddings either as decoration or confetti. They have been used in brewing for up to 3000 years according to Finnish records. Their original use in the brewing process was most likely as a preservative protecting against spoilage caused by bacterial growth, although hops also contribute to the flavour and bitterness of beer. So whether you choose to use hops in the decoration of your wedding or not, they will still most likely play a part in the celebrations!

VARIETIES

Humulus lupus. The specifics of your microclimate will affect the quality and characteristics of your hops. Many modern cultivars have been produced for specific locations and may not adapt well to every area. Your best chance of getting a variety that will thrive is to find a local friend or neighbour who has a healthy plant and propagate from them. Otherwise go to a garden centre and find a local variety. Unless you are looking into commercial scale production you will most likely be happy with what you find available locally.

GROWTH HABITS

Hops can climb to a height of 6m. The stout stems curl

around other plants or fences for support as they grow vertically. Once they run out of vertical support the hops will send out horizontal shoots and thicken sideways. Hops prefer a sunny position with rich, moist but well drained soil and are happy on a woodland edge. They can survive in the shade and even tolerate very dry or drought conditions providing there is plenty of humus incorporated into the soil. They are winter hardy, surviving minimum temperatures as low as -20°C (-4°F), although new growth in the spring is susceptible to damage from late frosts.

If you want to produce seed you will need both the male and female plants. They are wind pollinated, the ratio of one male to 5 or 6 females being sufficient for successful pollination. Female plants can also be propagated vegetatively in the absence of nearby males. This is usually the prefered technique if growing for use in beer as the seeds are undesirable when brewing. A simple method of propagation would be to cover a section of still growing stem with soil in a pot. You can do this multiple times along a single stem. New roots will develop with time at which point the ends of the stem leading into and out of the pot can be cut, leaving a couple of short lengths poking out. The roots will continue to develop and new shoots will be sent

up from the pot the following spring.

Hops die back in the autumn, storing their strength in the rhizome ready for a huge burst of growth the following spring. The roots can last up to 50 years, tirelessly sending up new shoots each year. Hops can grow as much as 50cm in length in a single week during prime growing season, rapidly refilling the space it occupied the previous year. They usually reach their maximum height by the end of June.

MAINTENANCE

When young you may want to weed around the emerging shoots, although I have never found this necessary as it is such a vigorous grower and quickly overwhelms any annual weeds.

Hops are susceptible to pest attack from the European corn borer, damson-hop aphid and the hop froghopper, amongst others. However this should not prove a problem to the small scale casual grower. Growing a wide variety of different plants in your garden will attract many different insects, some of them pest predators. This is your best defence if growing organically as the diversity of insects will enhance the ability of your immediate ecosystem to cope with any major influx of pests.

Both downy and powdery

mildew can affect your crop. In either case remove and destroy the affected parts.

Harvesting, Processing and Storage

Very small white pompom style flowers appear in July. Allow them to mature into strobiles which look a little like miniature papery bunches of grapes. Collect in late August or September and dry or use fresh. Dry the strobiles in the shade and store in a cool, dry place. When harvesting a quantity of hops dry them in a warm place such as an airing cupboard or a conservatory (but out of direct sunlight) as they spoil quickly if at all damp or if the drying process takes too long. Stems can also be collected for use at this point.

When handling the live stems of hops it is advisable to wear long sleeves and gloves as they can cause itchy welts or a rash in some people. This reaction is very rare but worth guarding against as it is rather unpleasant for the short period of time that it lasts.

USES

Food

The unfertilised seed heads are used as a flavouring and preservative in beer. If you do get seeds they are edible, leaving an oily but pleasant residue in the mouth.

The young shoots can be eaten raw, steamed, boiled or fried as a poor (or impatient) man's asparagus substitute. Only eat the shoots during spring and no later than May. The fleshy rhizomes can also be eaten but this appears to be only in times of desperate need as I have found no account of anyone actually doing this and have not tried it myself.

Medicine

The strobiles are the only part that is used medicinally. Infuse and drink a cup 30 minutes before eating to aid digestion and improve appetite. The infusion can also be drunk to ease flatulence, colic, IBS, muscle spasms and cramps. It soothes the nerves, aiding nervous conditions, irritability, anxiety and tension headaches. Drunk regularly it can help stimulate menstruation and drunk before bed it will ease you off to a restful night's sleep. The taste becomes more bitter the longer it is left to brew, so don't infuse for too long or sweeten with some honey. You can also make a sleep pillow from the strobiles which, when left close to the head while sleeping, will bring a restful night for infants, children and adults.

Avoid drinking the tea if suffering from depression, pregnant or breast feeding.

CLOTHING

Fibre can be obtained from the stems and woven into a coarse cloth which is similar to hemp in texture and appearance but not as stong. The fibres are quite coarse but have a good length, much longer than hemp. Unfortunately the fibres are very difficult to separate and the stems require soaking over an entire winter before they can be used, making it a very drawn out process.

GARDEN

Hops can provide great shade during the summer, climbing up and over pergolas, arches and other structures.

Despite dying back in winter hops can provide an excellent cover for unsightly fences and walls during the summer months.

Waste left over from processing hops is high in nitrogen and so is a good addition to the compost or can be used directly on the soil as a mulch.

MISCELLANEOUS

A brown dye can be obtained from the leaves and flower heads.

Livestock will eat hops.

The flowers can be dried and used as biodegradable confetti.

Flowering lengths of hop can be used either fresh or dried for decoration around the home and increasingly for rustic, natural themed weddings. If you hang the lengths when fresh and leave them for a period of time they will dry in situ, so you can leave them hanging for as long as you please or until they start to degrade naturally.

Lengths of stem can be woven into rustic baskets. They will become rather brittle on drying, so either use fresh or soak before using. If you have used them fresh the stems will shrink a little as they dry, affecting the tightness of your baskets' weave, something perhaps with which to experiment.

Fibres can be made into sackcloth.

Fibres from the stems can be used to make paper.

LIME
(Tilia spp.)

LIME WAS GREATLY valued by the romans who knew it as *the tree of a thousand uses*. Lime trees provide well revered folk medicine and have a liberal dose of associated legend. It is said that falling asleep beneath the shade of a lime will result in the sleeper being magically transported to the land of the faeries. This has yet to happen to me under a lime but I'm ever hopeful!

Lime trees often end up hosting mistletoe which can be a mixed blessing as mistletoe itself is a semi-parasitic species which, despite being capable of photosynthesising itself will also divert energy and nutrients from its host. In return it does however provide valuable forage in the form of its leaves, young shoots and fruits to a wide variety of bird and animal species. It is also traditionally used as a Christmas decoration under which you may be able to procure a kiss from your sweetheart!

Aphids love this tree so avoid parking beneath one or your car will end up very sticky - trust me, I know! Due to lime's tolerance of pollution they are often the tree of choice to line suburban streets, so choose your parking spot wisely.

Lime provides a soft, pale, lightweight timber that darkens over time. The softness of lime wood and its fine, straight grain make it relatively easy to carve and work with. It's not particularly durable but doesn't tend to warp or taint, a characteristic which makes it a favourite for kitchen utensils.

VARIETIES

American lime *(Tilia americana)*

Broad leafed lime *(Tilia platyphyllos)*

Common lime *(Tilia x europaea)*

Small leafed lime *(Tilia cordata)*

Other common names for lime are linden blossom and basswood (in the USA). The different varieties of lime are typically rather tricky to tell apart.

GROWTH HABITS

Being a woodland tree it will grow in relatively shady conditions, although it does enjoy full sun. In optimum conditions *Tilia platyphyllos* can grow to a height of 40m with a trunk diameter of up to 1.8m and the branches can sprawl to cover around 15m. It will grow in most soil types and tolerates nutritionally poor soil although it does need moisture and will not do well in very dry conditions. It can tolerate strong winds but

not the salty spray of coastal areas. Insect pollinated, this tree attracts plenty of insects and wildlife. The tree is frost hardy, surviving temperatures as low as -30°C (-22°F), although the leaves will fall shortly after the first serious frost in autumn.

Lime is difficult to propagate from the seeds which ripen in October. It can take up to 8 years to germinate and even the most patient of growers will no doubt have given up by then. However, once you have a tree they can live up to 1000 years. You may have more luck propagating from one of the suckers which you will usually find growing in abundance from the base of the trunk. Remove suckers during the winter dormant season with as much root intact as possible. Replant your sucker as soon as possible and encourage it with regular water and protection, especially over the first winter.

Coppice in a 10 year rotation to ensure plenty of young leaves over a long season for eating. Coppiced lime produces long, straight poles. A rotation of 25-30 years will produce good sized poles for turnery, furniture making and fuel wood and will produce an average of 2.5 tonnes of dry wood per hectare/per year.

MAINTENANCE

Give a layer of compost

around the base of the tree each autumn for the first few years to help your tree get established. Otherwise Tilia requires very little maintenance, just the removal of the odd dead twig or branch. They can, however, tolerate heavy pruning and you will often find them lining suburban pavements, radically cut back from time to time as the local authority sees fit.

Protection from browsing deer may be necessary if there is a large local population with access to your land.

Harvesting, Processing and Storage

Flowers should be collected along with the attached bracts when newly opened in mid summer. Choose a dry day. Flowers must be thoroughly dried in the shade before storing them in an airtight container. The flowers should not be kept for longer than a year as after this time they may begin to develop narcotic qualities.

Leaves can be harvested for eating from April until September but go for the young leaves as these have a better texture and are tastier.

USES

Food

Young lime leaves can be used as an alternative to lettuce throughout late spring and summer.

Honey made from the nectar of lime flowers is highly prized and considered by many as the best honey you will find. The medicinal properties of the flowers remain in the resultant honey, making it both calming and beneficial to ingest when fighting an infection.

The sap of lime can be tapped (see p62) and drunk fresh or used as a sweetener.

The flowers and immature fruits can be mashed into a paste which is said to taste chocolatey.

Medicine

Infuse the inner bark and drink it to treat diarrhoea.

A lime flower infusion has a pleasant, mild and rather sweet taste, so unlike most herbal remedies it is generally an easy one for children to stomach. Drinking the infusion will help calm, soothe irritability and ease you off to sleep. In addition it helps soothe coughs, sweat out fevers and fight colds by boosting the immune system. It helps to reduce cholesterol levels, relax the blood vessels and hence is a preventative medicine for heart disease. The relaxing properties will also help with all kinds of nervous digestive disorders such as indigestion and IBS.

A soothing cough syrup can be made from the flowers. They can also be added to a bath or footbath to help reduce anxiety while relieving insomnia and tension headaches. These are both good ways of calming hyperactive or anxious children. Alternatively, the flowers can be stitched into a sleep pillow and placed by the head in bed to calm the nervous, the anxious and insomniacs, bringing calm and restful sleep to adults, childern and babies alike.

Lime flower by its very nature is a nervine and a mild sedative, so use it with caution if you need to be alert and avoid it if you are suffering from prolongued periods of fatigue. Avoid using lime flower continuously for prolongued periods.

CLOTHING

A tough fibre can be obtained by soaking the inner bark of American lime in water for several weeks. Once separated these fibres can be woven into yarn for making clothing.

FUEL

The wood takes 12 months to season and despite being a slow burning, relatively low quality firewood, it makes good charcoal.

HOUSEHOLD

The wood is favoured for making kitchen utensils and chopping boards as it is virtually odourless and will not taint food. Like all woods it is naturally antibacterial.

Lime takes stain well and also has good bending properties, making it a favoured wood for indoor furniture.

Bast fibres can be stripped from the inner bark and roughly woven to make the seating on stools and chairs.

GARDEN

The flowers provide good bee forage, and it is said to be the best tree for bee fodder. The leaves provide the primary food source for some caterpillar species too.

Lime is known as one of the best trees for improving soil fertility because the fallen leaves rot easily, allowing all the nutrients to be absorbed by the soil. If you want to use the recycled fertility from the leaves in another area of your garden simply sweep them up and store them in a black bag, adding water to moisten them. They should have rotted fully after a year producing a dark, rich leaf mould that can be scattered where needed.

Being wind tolerant lime makes a great hedge or shelter belt tree.

Miscellaneous

Fibres found in the underbark have many uses. The best fibres are usually found on trees with trunks whose diameter is between 15 and 30cm, the size you would expect on a 10 year rotation coppice. Small leafed lime is most commonly harvested for these fibres although all lime species will have useable bast fibres present. The resulting fibres are generally too coarse to be made into clothing but will make strong and durable ropes, mats, baskets and fishing nets. Harvest branches or trunks in summer, strip the bark and soak it in water for up to 6 weeks to allow retting to occur. During the retting process individual bast layers separate and warmer conditions will speed up the process. Fibres from bark harvested in early spring will separate more easily, without the need for retting. Cordage made from lime bast is inherently pliable and resistant to decay. It has limited water absorbency, low extensibility and a low specific weight[23]. Incredibly lime cordage is also nearly 50% stronger when wet than dry, making it ideal for use in wet conditions. Bast from trees older than 15-20 years will be more coarse, stiff and less durable than that separated from younger branches or trunks.

The fibres can also be used to make paper. To do this you will need to harvest some small stems or thin branches during the growing season (spring or summer). The leaves will first need to be stripped before the stems are steamed. Remove them from the steam once the inner and outer bark can be separated. Retain the fibrous inner bark and cook it for two hours with lye or wood ash, rinse thoroughly, beat the mushy fibres and lay it out to dry. Your paper will have a beige tinge.

If you are not using the suckers to propagate new trees they can be used for basket making.

The timber has been traditionally used to make beehives, especially valued because it does not taint easily.

The wood is good for turnery and carving.

If you have a large section of felled trunk take advantage of the wood's light weight and make a dugout canoe!

The fresh leaf is palatable to livestock, making it a useful animal forage providing a bit of diversity to the diet. The leaves can also be dried and made into hay to provide food in the winter months.

Lime trees cast good shade and so provide a great spot for a picnic on a roasting mid summer's afternoon.

Rinsing your face regularly with a cool lime flower infusion will have a slight bleaching action, reducing the impact of freckles and blotches of discoloured skin. Soak a cotton wool pad in a cool lime flower infusion and place it over closed eyes. Leave it for between 10 and 30 minutes and it will reduce the appearance of dark circles under the eyes.

Rinse clean hair regularly with a jug of lime flower infusion to condition the hair, leaving it soft and shiny.

NOTES

23. T. Myking et al "Lime Bast Cordage in Northern Europe" Agroforestry News Volume 13, Number 3, May 2005, 5.

MONKEY PUZZLE
(Araucaria araucana)

I HAVE ALWAYS loved this strange and alluring tree since first seeing a lonely specimen as a child. I think it was the form of this striking tree and the very open habit of the spiked, spiralling branches that first enchanted me. There is fossil evidence dating the araucaria species back to the time when dinosaurs roamed the earth. It has even been suggested that the spikey, tough, scale-like, triangular leaves grew that way to prevent huge prehistoric herbivorous foragers chewing on its leaves!

It is the national tree in its native Chile where it grows in mountain forests. The conservation status of this unique tree is described as 'vulnerable' but luckily it is now a protected species in Chile. The land it covers is eagerly coveted by land owners and it is not unknown for arsonists to attack some of the few remaining stands of this magestic tree so that the land can then be used for other purposes. It is also protected in Argentina where the majority of their remaining trees are fortunately within the boundaries of national parks. International trade in monkey puzzle trees, seeds and products is prohibited due to its listing by CITES (the Convention on International Trade in Endangered Spieces of Wild Fauna and Flora). The trade resitriction is in place to protect the tree.

Growing a monkey puzzle tree can perhaps be viewed as an exercise in extreme patience or as a gift to your children, or perhaps more realistically grandchildren, as it takes many, many years to produce its edible seed. The seed of the monkey puzzle has, however, been a staple food for the indigenous people in parts of southern Argentina and Chile for hundreds if not thousands of years. Indeed the people of one tribe are known as *Araucanos* named after the monkey puzzle or *Araucaria*. Alongside the seed forming a valuable part of their diet, these people also prize the timber highly. A local name within South America for the monkey puzzle is *penhué*, and an indigenous group, the *Pehuenche*, which literally translates as 'people of the penhué', are again named after it. The Pehuenche also enjoy a special relationship with the tree, using it ceremonially on their altars at harvest time and in fertility rites.

The tree produces a pine like resinous timber that is straight grained, fragrant, light and durable. The colour varies between trees but is pale yellow for the most part, although you will find some with darker browns, reds and greyish wood.

VARIETIES

Araucaria araucana

GROWTH HABITS

In the temperate rain forests of Chile and Argentina, monkey puzzle can grow to a diameter of 2m, a height of 50m and reach the ripe old age of 1000 years or more. In the UK climate they are unlikely to get any taller than a maximum of 30m with a diameter of around 1.5m and a maximum age of 180 years. Despite this smaller size the spread of the branches can reach up to 15m. Luckily it has an open canopy and casts little shade beneath which makes it suitable as part of an edible forest garden, allowing light to penetrate and other fruit or nut trees to be productive below its architectural spiney branches.

Being a forest tree monkey puzzle prefers filtered sunlight, although it can grow unshaded as long as it is protected from long, hot, dry spells. It survives for longer in wetter areas and thrives when growing in deep, moist, well drained soil with a slightly acid pH. It will survive down to temperatures of -20°C (-4°F) once established. It is hardy enough to grow well in coastal areas where it may be exposed to salty winds but interestingly will not thrive in areas of heavy atmospheric pollution, so plant well away from busy roads.

The seeds lose viability rapidly, so plant them while still fresh to have the best chance of germination. Stick the pointed end of the seed into your compost mix but do not cover, and leave ½ to a ¼ of the seed poking out. They take up to 2 months at an average temperature of 15°C (59°F) to germinate, so don't give up too soon! As it germinates the seed will push itself out of the compost, coming to rest on the surface as a shoot develops above and roots below. Do not be tempted to push the seed back into the soil. This is normal, and pushing it back in will damage the delicate young roots. If the conditions dip below the necessary 15°C minimum then protect your pots in a cold frame or greenhouse. The root system on seedlings is very delicate and doesn't like being disturbed, so use a pot large enough to take a few years' growth, then plant out in the place where you intend it to stay, thus keeping root disturbance to a minimum. They will need some protection over the first winter to ensure survival.

Monkey puzzle can also be propagated from epicormic sideshoots. This should be done in May or June and they should spend their first months in a greenhouse or cold frame. An epicormic bud is a dormant bud found on the main trunk.

A normal sideshoot, when removed, will not develop roots and produce a new tree. Knowing the sex of the tree that you are taking cuttings from is the only way of being sure of the sex of your new tree until cones are produced 20 to 40 years later! That fact alone makes it worthy of attempting to propagate at least a few new trees by this method.

Being a slow growing tree you are looking at a maximum increase in height of around 35cm each year. It may take up to 5 years to really start achieving any noticable gain in height which is a good reason not to plant it directly into the ground as an enthusiastic arc with the strimmer may well remove the first couple of years' slow and steady growth in a heart beat and will for sure make you drop to your knees, tears welling.

Cones produced on the female trees contain up to approximately 200 seeds. The cones take 2-3 years to mature and once ripe they fall to the ground and open, making them easy to harvest. Ripe cones grow to the size of a human head, so if your tree is full of ripening cones it would be advisable to step aside as one of them on the back of the head could do some damage! The bad news is that it takes anywhere between 20-40 years to produce its first seed - as

I suggested, an exercise in patience. In addition, being a dioecious plant it needs both males and females to produce seed. A ratio of one male tree to every 5 or 6 females should be plenty. The difficulty when growing from seed is knowing whether you have males or females and it is a long time to wait to discover you only have one or the other.

The trees are wind pollenated and the male cone produces the pollen. Its cone which is cylindrical and almost cucumber shaped, grows to between 8 and 12cm long with a diameter of between 5 and 6cm at the base when the pollen is released. The female cones take around 18 months from pollination to produce ripe seed. In general female trees tend to be taller with thicker trunks. There have been reports of some trees displaying both male and female cones and you never know your luck; you may end up with one. If you have limited space enough for only one, seek out one of these monoecious individuals and try to find an epicormic sideshoot to propagate, ensuring that you will in time be able to enjoy nuts that have been pollinated and produced by your one tree alone.

Unlike any other conifer Monkey puzzle can be sucessfully coppiced. This is very useful if you are planning on using the distinctive wood for crafts rather than just patiently waiting for your first crop of tasty seeds.

MAINTENANCE

Monkey puzzle is susceptible to honey fungus so keep alert for any signs such as white fungal growth between the bark and wood or clumps of honey coloured toadstools. There is no treatment for this fungus and the best way to prevent its spread to other healthy trees is to remove and destroy the infected tree. This sounds drastic but the fungus will not survive in the soil without a tree to attach to and you may just end up saving other trees from the same fate.

It does not require much maintenance. Just love it and leave it to grow. As your tree gains height the lower branches will start to die back. It is best to remove these dead branches as they will take vitality from the rest of the tree. Approach the tree with caution as the triangular leaves are incredibly sharp and can cut through leather gloves.

HARVESTING, PROCESSING AND STORAGE

The seeds ripen between September and October. Once mature the monkey puzzle is a heavy cropper with the potential to produce a quantity of nuts greater than our native trees can manage. Unfortunately, as with hazel nuts, squirrels are equally keen to get their little paws on these valuable seeds despite the spikey leaves. Store the harvested seed in a cool, dry place away from direct light and they will remain good enough to eat for at least 9 months.

USES

FOOD

The seeds produced are a similar shape to an almond but up to twice the size with a smooth sheath. They have a soft and somewhat creamy texture and a flavour slightly reminicent of pine nuts. Rich in carbohydrates, fat and protein they make a valuable and dense food and although I have only had the pleasure of eating them once I do remember the seeds tasting quite delicious. Seeds can be eaten raw, boiled or roasted.

The seeds can be brewed and a popular local spirit is distilled from them in their native Chile.

MEDICINE

Wounds and ulcers can be treated by resin produced in the trunk and collected by making incisions in the bark. Sometimes you will find tacky deposits seeping from the bark

which can be used like pine resin to cover minor scrapes, cuts and bites upon which it will have an antibacterial action.

There are no reported cautions or contraindications for using monkey puzzle resin topically.

FUEL

The timber was used as fuel wood by the tribes people in its native lands until it gained protection by CITES. In reality unless you are experimenting with a monkey puzzle coppice or have a large old tree that is either dying or needs to be removed for another reason I would imagine it is highly unlikely that you would want to burn this timber. While currently considering the planting of a monkey puzzle glade myself, using the timber for fuel is the last thing on my mind.

BUILDING AND HOUSING

The fine grained timber from monkey puzzle has a high mechanical resistance and is also relatively resistant to fungal decay. These properties make it a valuable resource used to make strong and enduring roof beams.

The long, straight trunks can be milled into planks to make durable floor boards.

HOUSEHOLD

The pale coloured wood is attractive and makes beautiful furniture. It is especially prized in cabinet making.

GARDEN

The trees have a great presence with their evergreen curious looks and the great height they achieve with age, deserving a spot in any larger garden if just for aesthetic reasons.

MISCELLANEOUS

The strength and resistance to decay make it a popular wood to use around water and it is used in the construction of bridges, piers and boats, especially masts.

If you are into wood turning you can make really gorgeous bowls from monkey puzzle. The trunk has sets of lateral branches which emerge at intervals all the way up, giving a great pattern of knots all the way round your bowl.

Of course it could be used to make paper but this would seem like a huge waste for such a magnificent tree.

A seedling would make an inspired gift at the birth of a new baby, being mature enough to produce the edible seed by the time that child has a young family of its own!

If you have the patience and space to nuture seedlings you could develop a lucrative business. A tree of 30cm in height sells for around £25, 80cm for £50 and a 2m sapling goes for around £400 (at 2011 prices).

PUMPKIN
(Cucurbita spp.)

NATIVE TO THE Americas, the first evidence of pumkin cultivation comes from Mexico between 7000 and 5000BC. The name pumpkin generally refers to the tough, orange skinned members of the *cucurbit* family. It's really only the appearance of the skin that distinguishes them from squashes, to the amateur at least. One of my favourite characteristics of the pumpkin is how fast they grow on the day of germination. The first time I grew pumpkin I remember one morning the leaves had just begun to break the surface of the soil, then when a couple of hours later I went back for another look, amazingly the leaves were already totally clear of the soil and seemingly growing larger by the minute. It was a huge wrench to tear myself away from spending the whole day in the greenhouse cheering them on. I guess this would make them great fun for children to grow, especially as the interest continues when they set fruit and change daily in both size and colour. The child in me certainly never gets bored of checking them for the latest day's developments.

VARIETIES

There are two species with fruits that can be classified as pumpkins and each species has a great variety of different pumpkins, squashes and even gourds, all growing to a different size and shape and with different characteristics and flavour. Some of my personal favourites are:

Cucurbita pepo:

Lady Godiva - a variety grown for its sheathless, ready to eat seed and categorised as a winter squash by purists. The seeds are really tasty but the flesh is a bit watery and bland compared to other pumpkins.

Tom Fox - a compact traditional looking pumpkin which stores well.

Jack Be Little - only 8cm across and perfect for baking and stuffing and with an edible skin too!

Connecticut Field – the traditional type used for halloween lantern carving.

Cucurbita maxima:

Atlantic Giant - stores for 3-4 months and is the largest type of pumpkin. The biggest ever recorded weighed in at an incredible 450kg!!

Potimarron – grows to a much more manageable size and is reportedly the most tasty of pumpkins.

GROWTH HABITS

Pumpkin is a vigourous grower which loves deep, humus rich, fertile soil. If you have a greenhouse or polytunnel

the seeds can be sown in early spring and planted out once they have a few leaves and the threat of frost has passed. If you are planting directly into the soil wait until early summer before sowing. Soaking the seed in water overnight will speed up the germination process. Plant at a depth of around 4cm in rich soil leaving plenty of space between plants. The amount of space will depend on the variety but a general rule of thumb is about 1.8m between plants. Choose a sunny spot, protect from strong winds and incoporate plenty of well rotted manure or compost into the soil before planting.

Pumpkin is a fruit that grows on an annual vine but it is possible to create a perpetual pumpkin bed. Leave any fruits that have suffered damage from frost, nibbling mice or are just excess to requirement on the ground to rot, covering them with a thin mulch layer such as manure and straw or grow a green manure around them as a ground cover. The following year you will see new vines emerge. Protect them from slugs and snails at this point and you will have a whole new pumpkin bed for very little effort. This is how a friend of mine living in Auckland, New Zealand works and she now considers pumpkin and squash a weed, whereas I still treat each plant and new fruit with the tenderness of a newborn baby.

Maintenance

Pumpkins love water so give them plenty, especially during dry spells. Once your pumpkin has set fruit, feed them every couple of weeks. I use home made nettle or comfrey feed and failing that seaweed. As the summer comes to an end or when you are happy with the number of fruits on the vine, pinch out the growing tips. This will divert all the energy into the swelling fruits rather than producing more foliage and new fruits that will never reach maturity.

If your ground is damp or the autumn rain is setting in, raise your maturing pumpkins off the ground on an old tile or brick. If you don't have one available some straw will do. I always have a sprinkling of straw around anyway as a mulch on my beds to keep away weeds and hold moisture in the soil.

You will need to be extra vigilant for slugs when growing pumkins as they really seem to enjoy the sport of eating through the slim stems, especially when they are young and juicy. Last year they devoured all but one of the 20 or more different plants I had growing. Once they have set fruit mice may also become interested and take a nibble.

Pumpkins are susceptable to cucumber mosaic virus. If you see any signs of this disease your only option is to destroy the plant, hopefully preventing it from spreading to other individuals.

Harvesting, Processing and Storage

Pumpkins ripen in autumn. You will instinctively know when to crop them as their colour will be rich, the foliage dying back and the stems splitting. Although it is preferable to allow your pumpkins to reach maturity whilst still attached to the vine, if a heavy frost is forecast you will need to bring them in. If you do have to bring them in early leave them on a window sill for a couple of weeks to finish the ripening process and harden off the skins. Depending on variety they will store from several weeks to several months. One winter I went away in late December, already a couple of months after harvest, leaving a stack of 'Tom Fox' pumkins in my back bedroom on a shady window ledge. When I returned in March I was delighted to find that they were all still good to eat. Since then I have incorporated growing pumpkins as an essential part of my strategy for making it through the 'hungry gap' without getting too hungry! Pumpkins will store for longer if kept in a cool, dry place and some varieties will store for up to 9 months.

Seeds can be collected from any pumpkin you prepare to eat. Just rinse any pulp from the seeds and spead them out to dry for a week before storing in an airtight container in a cool, dry place. Select the largest and most healthy looking seed and save it to plant next season.

USES

FOOD

Pumpkin seed oil is produced from cold pressing the seed. It produces a dark, thick fragrant oil that has a very nutty taste. When consumed raw this nutritious oil is high in vitamins A, B2, B3, betacarotene, potassium, magnesium and zinc. The high zinc content will help hold back the development of grey hairs and is benefitial for prostate problems. It is also high in essential fatty acids, omegas 9, 6 and 3. Once pressed keep the oil in a dark glass bottle away from sources of heat and light and it will last for up to 2 years.

The flowers can be eaten fresh directly from the vine and make a most flamboyant edible garnish. Some people do strange things like cover them in batter and deep fry them, but that's not for me. I prefer their delicate taste and texture when fresh. The leaves can also be eaten but are a little tough and sometimes spiney, so you will need to

cook them first. Either steam them or use in place of other greens.

The flesh of pumpkin can be eaten in all manner of ways, from a healthy mash where it is cooked then mashed with raw garlic and olive oil, to soups, pies and curries. The flesh can also be eaten raw but it is quite hard to eat in chunks, so grate it into salads or as a topping for risottos and other cooked dishes. For the novelty factor you can bake pumpkin whole. Just cut off the lid, scrape out the seed and add some ingredients as a filling before replacing the lid and baking for about 1½ hours. When serving scrape the perfectly cooked flesh from the insides of the skin and distribute it between the assembled plates. This is a great trick for dinner parties but remember to always bake it on a dish to catch spillage and in case of a split in the skin.

The seeds are really tasty but the white outer sheath needs to be removed, revealing the dark green seeds inside before eating, unless you have grown a variety with 'naked' seed such as Lady Godiva which produce naturally sheathless seed. Eat them raw or toasted and tossed in salads. I like to make a savoury pâté with them. First soak 2 measuring cups of seed in water for several hours before draining. Then mix them with a bunch of fresh herbs, a teaspoon of crushed garlic and a dash each of lemon juice, olive oil and tamari in a blender until the consistency is creamy. This will keep in the fridge for 48 hours and is great on crackers or toast and as a side dish or a dip for crudités.

Pumpkin seed butter is delicious and can be made either with an attachment for a specialised juicer or in a dedicated seed or coffee grinder. Use raw seed and if the crushed seed comes out a little dry, try adding some cold pressed oil a little at a time to give the prefered consistency. You may also choose to add a little sea salt to taste. Make it in small batches and store in the fridge. It will keep for a month or more but do smell it before eating to check it has not gone rancid.

Dehulled pumpkin seed can be sprouted for adding to salads and raw dishes. First soak them for 8-14 hours, then leave for a day to sprout. Unfortunately they are a rather tricky seed to sprout and all of my attempts so far have left me with a rather disgusting and bitter tasting mush. It is however said to be possible, so have a go and good luck!

MEDICINE

A decoction made from the seeds will ease prostate problems and gout. Eating the

seeds provides not only a tasty snack but additional health benefits. If you are eating for health then crush the seed in a coffee grinder first to be sure they are properly broken up so your body can absorb all the nutrients. Any crushed seed that you do not eat immediately must be stored in the fridge or they will soon go rancid. The seed are highly alkaline which benefits the whole body and will help treat acidosis of the liver and blood. Containing significant quantities of zinc and magnesium, both essential in the production of semen, they are particularly beneficial to men suffering from fertility problems including low sperm count and motility. Magnesium also benefits prostate problems and eating a handful of seed a day will help reduce an enlarged prostate. Eating seed daily will also benefit acne sufferers and will soothe bladder problems whilst guarding against the formation of bladder and kidney stones. Spend a day eating only seed paste to expel tapeworm, roundworm and other parasites. A poultice of crushed seeds can be applied to minor wounds, burns and chapped skin.

Eating the pulp will soothe an inflamed digestive tract whilst a poutice made from the pulp can bring relief to minor burns.

Eating the raw flesh helps guard against the development

of cancer, respiratory disease and heart problems.

Drink a flower infusion for prostate problems using 3 flowers per cup.

There are no reported cautions or contraindications for using pumpkin medicinally.

GARDEN

Pumpkin grows as a vine with searching tendrils that can be trained over frameworks and trellises to optimise space in smaller gardens. If you train it over a small frame close to the ground it can provide shade and preserve moisture for plants likely to bolt in the heat of summer such as coriander, rocket and lettuce which you can plant below. Alternatively you can train pumpkin to grow up the side of a shed and onto the roof, thereby using the otherwise wasted roof space. I have even heard of a woman who grows it over an arch in her garden, providing a beautiful feature and of course shade below.

Pumpkin is often grown in combination with beans and maize. This is a historic guild called 'The Three Sisters'. The first evidence of this growing alliance is in Mexico and dates back 700 years. The three plants complement each other, the maize providing height and support for the beans to climb up, the beans fixing nitrogen into the soil and the

pumpkins providing a living mulch to hold moisture in the soil and supress weed growth. It's an efficient way of getting several crops from a small patch of land whilst exploiting each plant's characteristics for the benefit of the others. In colder climates you may need additional support for the beans as they will grow more quickly than the maize. I put in a few bamboo canes for the beans but still enjoy the benefits of growing the three plants together in the same bed. Pumpkins do not grow well with everything, particularly potatoes, so keep them separate.

MISCELLANEOUS

Pumpkin seed oil is great to use on dry, mature and damaged skin. Used as a massage oil directly on the skin it has a firming and lifting effect and can help out with those ever worrisome thighs, buttocks and even breasts. It also has rejuvenating and deeply moisturising effects when used on the face but patch test it first as the strong smell may be overpowering to some people.

Mash pumpkin seed and mix it with olive oil to form a paste for use as a face pack to keep the skin soft. This paste will also reduce the appearance of freckles.

Mix crushed seed into pet food to help improve any digestive issues and condition coats.

If you have too many pumpkins for your own use livestock will happily feed on them.

Apply the pulp to the face and leave for at least 10 minutes before rinsing off to improve the appearance of problem skin. It will help clear spots, pimples and acne.

One of the most famous uses of pumpkins is to scoop out the insides and carve grizzly faces in their skin, placing a tea light inside for use as a halloween lantern. If you are doing this don't forget to use the flesh to make a warming pumpkin soup for any trick or treaters in your family to come back to.

Gourds are the hard shelled fruits of some species of the *Cucurbita* family. Some can be eaten when young but on the whole they are grown for decorative purposes. I don't know anyone who has taken the time to grow gourd intentionally, although I do know a few who grew it from seed thinking they were pumpkins. If you do end up with a crop of gourd, intentionally or otherwise, they are actually quite useful. Crop the fruits before the first frosts and leave them on a sunny window ledge to dry out. Depending on the shape you can then use them as maracas (the dried seed

inside will provide the rattle) and they have been used to make ceremonial rattles this way in some cultures. To make a beautiful set of drinking vessels cut the tops off, scoop out the insides and leave to dry. If you have a long necked variety cut it into a ladle shape with the neck forming the handle. Dry it and use for serving soups or stews. All shapes make great containers for jewelery, trinkets and keepsakes. Decorate the outside by carving patterns, being careful not to press hard enough to go all the way through the skin. Then cut the top off. You can make a waved edge so it will fit snugly back on without sliding off too easily. Do all the carving and cutting and remove the seeds before it dries or it may become too brittle and shatter.

QUINOA
(Chenopodium quinoa)

QUINOA IS A native of the Americas and has been cultivated for at least 5000 years. It has been a staple grain for the peoples of the Andes from the time of the Inca and perhaps before. It was known to the Inca as *la chisaya mama,* 'the mother grain'. Grown widely across the mountainsides of Peru, Bolivia and Chile, it can also be successfully grown elsewhere and considering all of its attributes is worthy of a try in your own backyard. Quinoa has great potential with the possibility of being able to outcrop cereal grains in parts of Britain.

In folklore the seed of quinoa was given to the people of the altiplano by the sacred kullku bird as a gift from the heavens. The seed was believed to impart stamina, heightened psychic abilities and enabled the user to transcend into other deeply spiritual planes during meditation.

VARIETIES

Chenopodium quinoa
There are many different cultivars available for different conditions. Cahuil, Dave, Rainbow (produces good seed even in damp conditions) and Temuco are all suitable for growing in the UK.

GROWTH HABITS

Related to both pigweed and lamb's-quarters, quinoa is a hardy plant that can withstand drought and, depending on variety and growing conditions, can reach a height of 1.5m. It prefers rich, well drained, alkaline soil in a sunny position but will tolerate slightly saline soils with low levels of fertility. It will do best in a position where day time temperatures rarely exceed 32°C (90°F) and where nighttime temperatures remain cool. It can be sown outside at a depth of about 1cm in late spring. When planted in pots it can be better protected from slug and snail damage but if the soil temperature remains much above 15°C (60°F) at night they will not germinate. Germination should occur within 3-5 days. Optimum spacing for seed production is 15cm between plants. Add any thinnings to your salad bowl. Once established it can endure drought conditions, mild frosts and moderate winds, although it will not tolerate maritime exposure. The quantity of seed produced can be compared to commercial grain crops, achieving around 6 tons per hectare in the UK.

Quinoa seed may be sucessfully grown as a grain substitute even in small spaces due to the large yield from each plant. The seeds are coated with saponins making them unpalatable to birds which in essence ensures the majority of the harvest will be collected by you and not our little beaked friends.

MAINTENANCE

Quinoa is generally a low maintenance crop requiring very little watering even during dry spells, although a little weeding when young will remove competition and allow the quinoa to grow unhindered. As the seed heads mature and gain weight you may need to stake the plants or they could topple or be damaged by high winds.

HARVESTING, PROCESSING AND STORAGE

It will have flowered and be ready for cropping by late August or September. Once the leaves have fallen and the seed has started to fall freely from the flower heads, cut the stalks and lay in the sun over sheets of paper. After a few warm, dry days beat the stems and the seed will fall onto your paper. Any rain that falls onto your drying seeds may cause them to germinate so be vigilant and bring them under cover if necessary. To remove any detritis amongst the seed simply pass it through a loose meshed garden sieve and then winnow in the wind. Store the dry seed in an airtight container in a cool, dry place and they will remain good to eat for several years.

USES

FOOD

Quinoa seed is richer in protein than any grain, the average protein content being 16.2%, although depending on variety it can be as high as 20%[24]. Wheat is the only grain that comes close to this content. Quinoa contains all of the essential amino acids and is especially high in lysene for which soya is famed. It's also high in phenylalanine, tyrosine, cystine and methionine, giving it a similar amino acid portrait to cow's milk[25]. It has more than double the calcium and phosphorus content of wheat and much more iron on a weight to weight basis, leaving white rice and maize completely out of the competition[26]. Always soak and rinse before cooking to remove the saponins.
It is easy to cook and with its mild flavour is good for thickening soups and stews, or used as a grain alongside curries and other hot sauces. Cooked then cooled it can be combined with raw vegetables to make a salad in the style of tabouleh or rice salad. It is also popular at breakfast time as a porrige substitute. Unlike the majority of grains it remains alkaline after cooking and hence is great to eat for health as it helps keep the body's internal systems alkaline whilst keeping disease and degenerative conditions at bay.

Quinoa can be sprouted but make sure it still has its outer sheath. This is bitter tasting and so is most often removed in processing before it reaches the supermarket shelves. Start by soaking overnight and within 24 hours the white tail of the sprout will be noticeable. Rinse and drain a couple of times daily and within 2-3 days the shoot will have a hint of green and be ready to eat. As with cooking it remains a little crunchy even after sprouting. If you let the tails grow too long they will become increasingly bitter. I use it to bulk up salads and, as with cooked quinoa, as a bulgar wheat substitute in tabouleh.

Grind it into a gluten free flour for making breads and biscuits. The flour can also be used like rice flour and as a thickener in soups, sauces and gravies.

The seed can be fermented to make a kind of beer.

The leaves can be eaten as a vegetable. Use young leaves raw in salads and older leaves can be steamed or cooked as a spinach-like substitute. If eating the leaves raw only use a few at a time as they can upset your stomach when eaten in volume. Leaves can also be juiced with other fresh vegetables for a nutrient rich, health giving beverage.

Medicine

Cooked quinoa seed can be applied to the skin as a poultice to help with particularly bad bruising.

High in calcium, eating the seed regularly will act as a preventative medicine against osteoporosis whilst some of its other other properties will help guard against arteriosclerosis.

Quinoa does contain oxalic acid so eat it with caution if you suffer from rheumatism, arthritis, gout, hyperactivity or kidney stones.

Fuel

The stalks can be burned to provide heat or processed into bioethanol to fuel petrol engines (see p172).

Garden

Save the water you have soaked seed in prior to cooking and use it to spray over plants. The saponin content will deter aphids and other insects.

It is an attractive plant to grow with the seed heads coming in an array of colours from green through yellow and orange to red.

Miscellaneous

Use saponin from water used to soak seed as a soap.

The whole plant, or the parts you have no other use for, can be fed to poultry, cattle, pigs, horses and sheep.

Dyes ranging from gold to green can be obtained from the whole plant.

Notes

24. Steve Meyerowitz, *Sprouts The Miracle Food: The Complete Guide To Sprouting* (Sproutman Publications, 1983), 77.

25. Ibid.

26. Ibid., 78.

SPELT
(Triticum spelta)

SPELT IS ONE of the oldest cultivated grains with its origins in Iran dating back to around 5000BC. Spelt is a sub-species, or perhaps more accurately an ancient precursor, of modern wheat. It lost favour as farming became more mechanised in the 1800s, as being comparatively tough it was more difficult for the threshing machines to deal with. In addition spelt has a lower yield than more modern varieties of wheat despite being able to survive in poor soils and remain standing even during torrential downpours. Being abandoned so long ago by industrial farming, spelt has been largely ignored, avoiding much manipulation by modern breeding techniques. This has left spelt with many of its original traits and nutritional profile intact – having more protein than modern wheat with gluten that is characteristically more brittle and soluble, making it easier to digest and suitable for consumption by some people who suffer wheat sensitivies. Spelt as a whole plant has many uses besides the grain itself, including building materials and medicine.

VARIETIES

Triticum aestivum var. spelta
Triticum spelta

GROWTH HABITS

Seeds remain viable for up to 5 years and once planted will usually germinate within

3 days, taking a further 110-130 days to reach ripeness. Spelt prefers moist, sandy soil in full sunlight. Spelt should be planted with the husk still on at a density of around 200-300 grains per m² and at a depth of no more than 4cm. It can either be planted in the autumn so that it becomes established before the bulk of the frosts arrive and will then continue to grow at a slow rate throughout the winter for an early summer harvest, or plant it in early spring when it will grow much more quickly and be ready for harvest around mid to late summer. It is frost resistant and the tough husk provides natural protection for the tender grains as they develop on the plant, protecting them from pests and disease and making spelt naturally resilient and suited to organic growing methods. When the seeds germinate they have a somewhat prostrate growth habit which cuts down competition from weeds which are then further shaded as the spelt grows tall and strong.

In a conventional system the soil is tilled and the grain plants are still very small when their growth slows in the cold of late autumn. This leaves much of the soil bare making erosion a potential problem during winter rains. Growing at home you can intercrop your spelt, ie grow it through a perenial clover pasture or simply amongst other plants.

If you are growing it as a hobby and not for financial gain, experiment with your planting. Try giving a very wide spacing of say 60cm between each grain planted which will allow up to ten times the number of tillers (stalks) to grow on each plant than in a conventionally spaced planting, each tiller producing an ear of grain. You can also experiment with following the natural lifecycle of the spelt more closely and instead of planting in September shortly after the previous years growth has been cropped you could plant in June between your current growth. Crop the previous year's plants in August as usual leaving your new growth to really establish itself before the winter dormant season. The main danger is that your seed could try to complete its entire lifecycle before winter comes, although heritage seed will not tend to do this. What I have just described is more or less the theory behind the Bon Fils system which is described in much greater detail in Patrick Whitefields' *The Earth Care Manual*.

Sometimes the odd grain remains amongst the straw I use to mulch my beds and paths, so I end up with random spelt plants growing here or there. If left to grow these volunteers can be harvested alongside those purposely planted, adding extra ears for no more effort.

MAINTENANCE

Spelt is a grass so be careful not to weed out your seedlings or allow them to be choked by other grass species. It is quite low maintentance, thriving without the application of fertilisers even on poor soils. It needs little watering except during exceptionally hot, dry spells. Overwatering will cause the stalks to grow too tall and then fall over or *lodge.*

HARVESTING, PROCESSING AND STORAGE

Collect the grains in mid to late summer either in the evening or on a humid morning. Gather the seed heads as they dry on the plants but before full maturity and store in paper bags to finish the drying process. The grains are traditionally stored with the husks still on and the husks removed before use. The stalks can be harvested at the same time and hung to dry. Once dried the stalks can be baled for ease of storage.

USES

FOOD

In addition to having a higher protein content and being easier to digest than modern wheat spelt is also high in fibre, has a low gycaemic index, is rich in zinc, iron and B vitamins and contains mucopolysaccharides which are important for both blood clotting and stimulating the immune system. Once the outer layer of bran has been removed from the grain it resembles pearl barley and can be used in a similar manner to thicken soups and stews, added to herb rich salads or used instead of couscous or arborio rice in recipes. Spelt grain can be ground into flour and used in place of wholewheat flour in breads, baking and pasta. The grain can also be sprouted and added to salads.

MEDICINE

Spelt grass has amazing health giving benefits and is easy to grow. First remove the husks then soak in water overnight. Place them in a sprout bag or if you do not have one keep in a jar in a dark cupboard and rinse twice daily for three days. The next step is to get a seed tray with a couple of centimetres of compost lining the bottom. Scatter your seeds over the surface and then cover with an upturned seed tray. This will keep the light out as the seeds complete the germination process. Keep covered for around three days, misting or watering lightly if they start to dry out. After three days the seeds will have sprouted and should have fine roots. At this point you can remove the cover tray and leave them to grow in the light, watering occasionally. The grass will grow fast reaching 10cm or more in around 5 days and achieving a wonderful, vibrant deep green. Then cut a handful of the grass with scissors at the base of the stems and juice, drinking it as a shot on its own or combine with other vegetable juices if you find the flavour too strong. The grass will usually grow back, although not as thickly so that you can usually cut the whole tray twice before putting what's left in the compost and starting again. It is best to drink it at least a couple of hours after the last thing you ate and for this reason I tend to use it first thing in the morning. If you are using it for a serious health condition you may want to drink up to 3 glasses full throughout the day, but always give plenty of time to digest anything you have eaten first and leave at least 30 minutes before eating again.

The grass is a good source of calcium and is literally loaded with vitamins, minerals, enzymes, amino acids, chlorophyll and other nutrients. Drinking the juice will help your body eliminate toxins which is useful if you are embarking on a cleanse or have been exposed to drugs, pollution or a diet high in processed foods. It cleanses the blood, slowing the aging process and leaving you feeling energized. It helps to stimulate the liver, again assisting in the detoxification

process. It has a dilating effect on the blood vessels, improving circulation and as a tonic can help improve the heart's function. It's effective in treating anaemia, boosts the immune system, can help improve fertility and has an alkalizing effect on the blood which is essential for good health. It offers protection against the formation of free radicals whose presence is implicated in disease development and premature aging. The presence of both abscisic acid and B17 (laetrile) can help the body fight cancer. It will help to treat gastro-intestinal complaints such as constipation, diarrhoea, ulcerative colitis and peptic ulcers. In addition the function of the thyroid gland will be stimulated and normalised by regular ingestion of spelt grass juice. On a more social note drinking the juice regularly will help neutralize bad breath and body odour whilst reducing the presence of gas.

Gargle with the juice to relieve sore throats and freshen stale breath. Chew the fresh grass and keep in the mouth to soothe sore gums and treat pyorrhea. Use the diluted juice as a douche for cystitis and vaginal thrush[27]. To clear blocked sinuses drip several drops of juiced grass in each nostril and inhale.

A small glass of juice added to your bathwater or rubbed directly over the skin will stimulate circulation[28]. Apply to the skin for sunburn relief and to soothe and accelerate the healing of cuts, minor burns, boils, sores, skin ulcers, grazes, rashes, poison ivy, athlete's foot and insect bites. You can either dab the juice directly onto the affected area, soak a bandage in the juice and hold that against the wound or make a poultice from the pulped grass.

A tray of grass growing on a bedside table will increase oxygen levels and generate negative ions which can help insomniacs sleep[29].

Consumption of spelt grass causes the body to detox and during this process there may be some undesirable side effects such as headaches and nausea. Do not worry - this is a good thing as it means the toxins are leaving your body and the side effects will clear when the toxins have passed through. Build up use of spelt grass slowly to avoid experiencing too strong a detox reaction. Pregnant and breast feeding mothers should avoid wheat grass to protect their infant from the toxins that are being released.

FUEL

The straw can be fermented to make cellulosic ethanol and then used as a fuel to supplement or replace petroleum use (see p172).

Bales can alternatively be burnt in biomass burners to produce heat, energy and/or hot water.

BUILDING AND HOUSING

Any straw such as spelt with a length of between 90 and 110cm can be used for thatching, although straw that has been exposed to nitrogen fertilisers will be weaker and hence not have the longevity on your roof of an organically grown raw material. Trials in the West Country have shown spelt to be a good roofing material, whereas modern wheat varieties which have been bred to have short stalks are consequently unsuitable. This use of the straw has the potential to reverse the recent trend of importing thatching materials from as far afield as China.

The straw can be tightly baled and used for straw bale construction. Straw bales make environmentally sound, well insulated buildings that are relatively cheap and easy to erect.

Straw can also be mixed with clay based soil, water and a little sand to form what is known as cob. Many houses in Britain were built from cob prior to the 1800s. Cob building is experiencing a renewed interest as sustainable buildings are becoming more popular. It is slow to build with as the cob is added in layers anywhere from 15-90cm high and literally trodden into the wall. Each layer must be left to dry for 2 weeks before the next can be added. It is great fun but very hard and dirty work, especially when you get a little over enthusiatic with the depth of your 'riser' and watch several hours sweaty effort literally flop to the side and break off in front of your eyes! It is, however, a very cheap and sustainable way to make a durable house from the earth under your feet. One of the more fun things about buildings constructed in this way is that they can be any shape you like with curving walls, odd shaped windows and alcoves built in. You can make brick shaped cob loaves and use them to gradually build up your walls if you are working alone, as building with cob is somehow easier as a community activity. Well constructed cob is load bearing, meaning that you can make two storey buildings from it. As with straw bale construction cob walls provide excellent insulation from both temperature and noise. The walls will absorb heat during the day time and radiate that stored warmth back out during the colder evenings. It needs a good overhang from the roof to protect the walls from the elements and a breathable render, traditionally lime. One additional benefit of building with cob is that it is fireproof.

The long lengths of straw can be coated with just enough clay to get them to stick together. This technique is known simply as 'light straw/clay'. You can use it for internal walls but would need a timber frame or lattice to hold the material. It is again a good insulation against both temperature and sound.

HOUSEHOLD

Stalks can be made into compressed board used in making cabinets and other interior furnishings.

GARDEN

Straw can be used as a mulch in the garden. Strawberries love a layer of straw around their base and its presence is said to enhance the flavour of the berries. I often scatter straw on my beds between established plants to reduce the need for weeding and to hold moisture in the soil. I also tend to apply a deep layer of straw on top of newspaper, compost and manure when I am leaving a bed empty over winter before planting with the spring crop. The straw on top will be drawn down and incorporated into the soil by the action of earthworms, increasing the soil's organic matter content. At the same time it will protect the soil from the elements, hence reducing erosion due to rainfall run off, whilst keeping the soil surface warm and ready for the spring crops. In addition it acts as a barrier which prevents weed seed reaching the soil and germinating, removing the need for a big clearing job before the spring seeds can be sown. If, like me, you have a raised bed system try covering the paths with the kind of membrane usually used under gravel and top it with a thick layer of straw. I did this 2 years ago at minimal expense and have found virtually no weeds finding their way up through it, just a couple at the edges. This makes for weed free paths that are very comfy to kneel on whilst planting and weeding.

MISCELLANEOUS

Non-allergenic pillow fillings can be made from the grain. These were in fact recommended by Hildegard von Bingen in the twelfth century for people with neck and shoulder pains, possibly due to the grain's high silica content which helps prevent stiffness and muscle tension. If using it for such pains you can heat it in the oven at a low temperature before using. The pillow will retain the heat for up to 3 hours and can also be used to comfort and ease menstrual pains. Small air pockets remain between the grains which allows the pillow to mould itself to the shape of the sleeper's head whilst allowing free circulation of air and providing a comfortable night's sleep.

The grain can be used as an animal feed.

Oil pressed from spelt germ has a high vitamin E content and is a highly prized addition to skin and hair care products. Applying it directly to the skin can help improve the appearance of scarred tissue. Dabbing it around the eyes will help prevent premature wrinkles.

Feeding the fresh grass to hens will improve their condition. Finely chopping fresh grass into the food of domestic pets or adding a few drops of the juice to their drinking water will help improve their condition, especially if they are under the weather.

The grass juice can be used as a treatment for an itchy or scaly scalp and to return lustre and condition to hair. Rub some juice into your scalp and hair and leave it on for a couple of hours before rinsing.

Paper can be made from the stalks.

Straw bales can also be used as makeshift urinals for men at outdoor events. The straw will absorb the urine which in turn will accelerate the straw's breakdown. The straw can then be scattered as mulch or added to the compost pile.

Bales can of course also be used as temporary outdoor seating at summer events but don't do this with ones that have previously been utilised as urinals!

Notes

27. Ann Wigmore, *The Wheatgrass Book* (Avery, 1985), 91.

28. Ibid., xiv.

29. Ibid., 93.

STINGING NETTLE
(Urtica dioica)

STINGING NETTLE CAN be found on almost any bit of waste ground and often along hedgerows and country lanes. To me fresh nettle is one of the archetypal smells of spring. Walking along a green lane where all the trees are in bud and the air is thick with the rich, green smell of nettle is medicine in itself. For wild food and medicine foragers alike, nettle really has no equal and is one of our many native superfoods. Despite this, nettle is probably most famed and often disliked for its irritating sting and quite appropriately its name *urtica* derives from the latin 'to burn'. The leaves and stems are covered with hair like spines that can penetrate the skin and subsequently break off, releasing a cocktail of chemicals including formic acid. The stings are easily disabled in processing by crushing, steaming, boiling or soaking, so as long as you are prepared and protected whilst collecting these wonderful plants you should not suffer from their bite! Drying can also disarm the sting but I would still be cautious as their sting can remain loaded for quite some time.

Nettles have been widely used throughout history. The German army uniforms in World War II were spun from nettle fibres whilst the Romans who brought nettles to Britain almost 2000 years earlier did so to whip themselves with the stings, knowing that the rush of blood to the sting site would at least provide temporary relief from the cold conditions.

Varieties

Urtica dioica
There are other *urtica* species throughout North America and Europe that can be used in the same way as stinging nettle, however *Urtica ferox* (native to New Zealand) must be avoided as the sting is much more serious and in extreme cases can even cause death.

Growth Habits

Nettle is dioecious with both male and female plants and dangling flowers that are wind pollinated, producing many tiny seeds. They also spread by their ever eager exploring roots and it is these you need to be wary of if you are cutivating a small patch and want to restrict the area they cover. Nettle has been reported to have reached more than a staggering 2m in height, although in my experience it rarely grows above 1.5m tall. It prefers rich soil but will do well in most locations, enjoying full sun or partial shade. Nettle dies back in winter and is one of the first greens to poke through the earth in early spring.

Maintenance

If nettle wants to grow it will and there is very little you will need to do, so no watering or weeding needed. If you cut a patch back to the ground for use it will have grown back thick and strong within days during the growing season. If you want to restrict where it grows you will need to remove the creeping rhizomes. Luckily they remain relatively close to the soil surface so are easy to pull out.

Harvesting, Processing and Storage

Seeds are collected by cutting stems bearing plenty of seed and hanging them upside down to dry. Once dried run your hands down the inverted stems catching the falling seeds in a container placed beneath. I recommend wearing gloves for this process as although the stings are generally disarmed by drying, a few always remain to catch you off guard.

Leaves can be collected to be used fresh from March until late June. Cut the stems in spring and hang them to dry in small bunches out of direct sunlight in a warm, well ventilated place to provide good quality nettle tops for use when fresh nettle is out of season. Roots are best when collected in June or July and can be used fresh or split and dried thoroughly for later use.

Store dried nettle tops and roots in an airtight container away from direct sources of light. Use the leaves until spring when new fresh nettle tops start appearing, at which point discard your dried nettle into the compost and use fresh ones instead.

If harvesting for fibre wait until autumn as the foliage is dying off, just before they start to die and decay. If making coarse cordage or rope, take the stems and strip the stings by running gloved fingers down the length of the stem while squashing it flat. Split the stem open and scrape to remove the inner pith then follow the instructions for processing into cordage. If extracting the fibre to make fine weave cloth you will need to either ret the nettle and then comb out the fibres in a similar manner to flax (see p74) or collect some stems, remove the stings, split into strips and leave for a few days to dry. The fibres will now separate easily from the pith and can be combed to clean and separate them. Soak to soften the fibres before spinning into yarn. If you cannot spin simply take a small bunch of fibres at a time and twist them together by rubbing them on your thigh. Keep adding more fibres to increase the length.

USES

FOOD

Fresh nettle tops make a nutritious food containing high levels of vitamins A and C, iron, potassium, trace minerals and protein. Do not consume the leaves after mid June as they will become grainy, having developed a high level of oxalate crystals. This makes nettle, in essence, a seasonal springtime food. Many people use it like spinach or make soup with it. I like to throw it in the blender for blood nourishing smoothies, substitute it for basil in home made pesto or simply juice it along with some sweet tasting fruits or vegetables. Try it with beetroot for a real blood nourishing treat. The dried or fresh leaves can be added to any dish in place of other herbs but remember if they are fresh they will either need heating or crushing to disable the sting before you serve them to your dinner guests! Dried, crushed leaves add a mild salty flavour to a dish, so if you are avoiding adding salt to your food why not try this as an alternative. Once the leaves are no longer edible look out for the seed as once collected these are great lightly toasted and sprinkled over salad leaves, giving a nutty crunch. The seeds are high in omegas which will benefit and fortify menopausal women.

Vegetarian cheese fans may want to experiment with using nettle as a rennet to curdle milk and hence provide a substitute for animal derived rennet. There are two ways of doing it. You can either juice the nettle if you have a good quality leaf juicer or boil nettle for 20 minutes in a strong salt solution, then combine with the milk and proceed with your cheese making. Having only made cheese once I am no expert and in fact was rapidly demoted to the position of thermometer holder, so I'm afraid I cannot be more specific than this! Nettle leaf can also be used to wrap cheese to which it imparts a subtle flavour.

For those fond of a tipple you could always try making nettle beer or wine. A basic recipe for nettle beer is to take approximately 50 stems with leaves and boil them in 6 litres of water for 15 minutes. Leave to cool before straining, then stir in 750g of sugar and 25g cream of tartar until dissolved. Leave until tepid then stir in 7.5g of yeast and cover with a teatowel or cheese cloth, leaving it for 4 days while it ferments. Remove any scum that has accumulated on top, pour it into bottles and seal with corks. Leave for a month before drinking and serve chilled

MEDICINE

An infusion of nettle leaf is very cleansing and so will improve all kinds of skin conditions as they are often associated with a sluggish system. It also makes an ideal basis for a spring cleanse. Drink 3 cups daily for 3 weeks once fresh nettle is plentiful. This will kick start your sytem and clear out many of the toxins you may have accumulated on those cold, dark winter nights where activity has been limited and indulgence in rich food and drink has been plentiful. When making a nettle infusion leave it to brew for as long as possible. I often make it with cold water and leave it overnight as you get a much richer and stronger tasting medicine this way. Of course you will still get benefit from a usual 10-15 minutes in hot water and this would be a good place to start as when left a long time it becomes almost soupy and this may be too intense for beginners. It helps relieve gout, rheumatism, arthritis and kidney stones. It cleanses the liver and blood, is fortifying to convalescents and will help treat anaemia. It will support women entering puberty and experiencing the menopause. It dries up excessive bleeding including frequent nose bleeds, haemorrhoids and blood in stools and urine whilst reducing heavy menstruation. It relieves asthma, bronchitis, lung congestion, colds and flu. It will improve childhood and nervous eczema and as an antihistamine will moderate allergic reactions. Drinking it daily for one month before hay fever symptoms usually appear and while you experience them will reduce your suffering. Nettle also lowers blood sugar, blood pressure and elevated heart rate. It stimulates milk flow in breast feeding mothers and will help regulate sleep, appetite, moods, relieve anxiety and inhibit pain. It also acts as a mild antidepressant. An infusion can be gargled to relieve a sore throat and used as a mouthwash to reduce the pain of a sore mouth or mouth ulcers.

Dry leaves can be powdered and packed into the nostrils to dry up nose bleeds.

The sap from the stem is a remedy for its own sting and will equally relieve the pain and inflammation of other bites and stings. If the sap seems hard to obtain, juice the stem and leaves and dab that onto the affected area. Applied to the skin the juice will also soothe and heal eczema whilst drinking it regularly will improve asthmatic conditions.

A decoction made from the roots will ease kidney problems and water retention whilst reducing an enlarged prostate and relieving the associated problems. A tincture made from the roots will benefit prostate problems and coughs.

Use with caution if pregnant or breast feeding.

CLOTHING

Taller nettles have stronger fibres. The bast fibres are finer than those of hemp, allowing for a finer weave cloth to be created. Once you have a length of nettle yarn you can knit with it or weave it into fine cloth. Nettle makes fabric that is stronger than linen and once it has been through the wash a few times is also very soft.

FUEL

Any plant matter left over from other uses can be processed into bioethanol and used as a fuel in petrol engines (see p172).

HOUSEHOLD

Fine quality, durable sheets and tablecloths can be made from nettle fibre.

GARDEN

If you have a patch in your garden nettle will attract many kinds of butterfly, moth and other beneficial insect that will busy themselves with pollinating many of your other plants. In fact, over 30 species of insect feed on nettle and several species of caterpillar are dependent upon it, so a patch of nettle will enrich your local ecosystem. Some insects that are attracted to nettle also provide pest control in your garden, such as ladybirds who will in turn dine on aphids allowing some of your finer edible crops to grow unhindered. You may sometimes find that your nettles themselves become infested with aphids. Don't worry as this provides valuable food for birds until the seeds ripen which will then provide mealtime treats for our feathered friends. One species of aphid active early in the year is specific to nettle. This will attract aphid predators who will then hopefully rotate around your garden clearing up other aphids that arrive later on to feed on your food crops and flowers.

Cut nettle can be added to your compost pile but be careful not to include seeds or sections of root. Nettle has the action of accelerating your compost formation.

You can make a nitrogen rich feed from cut nettles, perfect for use on flowering vegetables and non sweet fruits such as tomatoes and cucumbers. Simply place some nettle in the bottom of a bucket, fill with water (preferably non treated, such as rainwater) and weigh down the leaves at the bottom of the bucket. I usually use a plate with a stone on it. Leave to brew for three weeks by which time you will have a very rich and stinky plant food ready for use. Strain off the plant

matter which can be added to the compost. To use it you will need to dilute one part nettle to ten parts water. I do this roughly by adding a yoghurt pot full of nettle brew to my watering can which I then top up with water. Now all you need to do is get to work feeding all your food crops once a fortnight. This nitrogen rich feed can also be used for houseplants but don't forget to dilute before use and only use during the growing season.

Spraying plants with a little of the undiluted fermented nettle brew described above will deter aphids.

Cut nettle can also be used as a weed supressing, moisture retaining mulch around your food crops that will of course impart its nitrogen rich blend of minerals to the soil as it decomposes.

MISCELLANEOUS

Rinsing the hair and scalp with a nettle infusion will improve the condition of dandruff and an otherwise dry, itchy, flaky scalp. Using the rinse regularly will also stimulate the blood circulation, encourage hair growth and improve hair condition. Before the end of the growing season make a nettle tincture (see p179). This will allow you to keep using this treatment in the winter. To use mix 3 teaspoons of the tincture in a jug of water and use daily to rinse the hair.

For your hair and scalp to benefit from nettle's properties without using a rinse, make a herbal shampoo instead. Make 1 litre of a strong infusion using distilled water. You can add other herbs such as rosemary for their purfume and beneficial properties. Strain the infusion and add 150g of grated castile soap. Bring to the boil and stir constantly until the liquid is clear. Remove from the heat and beat briefly before pouring into bottles for storage. Use as needed.

The leaves provide a green dye and the roots a yellow one. Choose your colour and fill a pan with either leaves or roots, top up with water, cover and boil for an hour. Strain off the plant matter and place your fabric in the water, leaving it for up to 24 hours depending on how strong a colour you want. It will then be necessary to fix the colour. Add the fabric to a pan containing 3 parts cold water to 1 part vinegar, bring to the boil and simmer for an hour. Finish by rinsing your newly dyed garment thoroughly until the rinse water runs clear.

Goats will browse on fresh nettle, seemingly unaffected by the stings. Dried nettle can be fed to cattle in with hay and is said to improve milk production. Chickens also seem to benefit from the addition of dried or boiled and mashed nettle to their diets where it helps prevent coccidiosis in chicks and will extend an adult's egg laying season[30]. Dried nettle and nettle seed will benefit horses, improving digestive troubles, providing a cold remedy and giving a glossy coat.

Hanging a bunch of nettle in your kitchen to dry for infusions will have the added benefit of detering flies.

Juicing nettle and rubbing it liberally on leaky wooden tubs and barrels will make them watertight[31].

Fibre from the stem can be made into a strong twine, string or rope. Once the fibres have been extracted choose your method for making cordage. Either split the stem into four pieces and plait them together or just take a length of the fibres and twist both ends in the same direction until you get a kink in the middle, then twist it back on itself and you will have a two-ply string. For thicker lengths and rope, twist together bunches of fibres and then plait into three-ply cord. The cordage produced is very strong and can be used straight away or stored for later use. If storing for later use soak first to restore flexibility. Use finer cordage for weaving into sack cloth or for making fishing nets.

You can weave the stems into rustic baskets, mats and bags

but remember to first strip off the stings!

Paper can be made from nettle fibre. Cut the stems into lengths of around 2cm then boil and soak to clean and soften the fibres. Remove the fibres and spread over paper making frames and leave to dry.

Notes

30. Piers Warren, *101 Uses For Stinging Nettles* (Wildeye, 2006), 57.

31. Ibid., 65.

SUNFLOWER
(Helianthus annus)

SUNFLOWERS ARE NATIVE to the Americas where there is evidence of their cultivation dating back at least 4000 years. They were introduced to Europe by Spanish explorers in the 1500s, eventually making it to Russia by the 1700s where they became incredibly popular and new disease resistant strains with high oil yields were selectively bred. The extracted oil was favoured in Russia and eastern Europe as it continues to pour well even in cold conditions unlike many other oils.

Sunflowers are said to bring fertility to women who eat the seed and are also said to bring wisdom and luck to those who choose to grow these giants. You can probably explain both of these pieces of folklore with science as the oil from the seed is high in omega 6, an EFA which benefits brain health, fertility and sex drive (in both men and women).

I cannot look into the centre of a sunflower head without my hairs standing on end as the spiralling pattern made by the maturing seed touches something deep inside of me. The pattern produced by the closely packed seeds is a representation of the Fibonacci sequence, a beautiful example of sacred geometry and a natural balance between symmetry and asymmetry. While the leaf and stem are growing the flower heads have a very noticable heliotropic movement, following the sun's daily arc across the sky from east to west, adding just a bit more magic to this plant's awesome presence.

VARIETIES

There are an estimated 67 species and 19 subspecies of sunflower growing in the wild accross North America alone! Traditionally the flowers have yellow petals and dark centres, although now many different cultivars are available with petals from lemon through reds to burnt oranges and almost browns with centres just as variable, from pale greens and yellows to almost black. Depending on variety you will either get small black seed which are oil rich or larger seeds that come encased in a black and white striped hull. These are the type most often grown for eating.

Dwarf Russian produces a reliable crop of edible seed.

Rostov has black seeds that can be pressed for oil.

Russian Mammoth is grown primarily for the edible seed, produces between 1000-5000 seeds per head and reaches a height of up to 3.7m.

GROWTH HABITS

Sunflower is an annual which, depending on variety, can grow to anything from 0.45 to 5m in a single season. They are drought resistant but will fare better with regular watering. They prefer deep, rich, well draining soil in a sunny spot, although they will tolerate light shade. Sunflower will not survive in salty or waterlogged soils. Sunflowers are hungry feeders so it is best to rotate them around your plot to avoid depleting the soil.

Plant the seed in late spring or early summer at a depth of around 2cm with a spacing of around 30cm between plants. They will take up to 2 weeks to germinate and can take a light frost in the early stages, although it is best to plant them when all danger of frost has passed. I normally start sunflowers off in a greenhouse so that they can get a good start before being planted out in early summer. Once established they are very low maintenance, growing rapidly with minimal work. They flower from July to September with the seedheads maturing during September and into October. When the flowerheads have matured if you allow some seed to fall to the ground you will have new seedlings springing up the following year for very little effort on your part.

The flowers are pollinated

by bees and depending on variety you may get upwards of 1000 seeds per flowerhead. Sunflowers grow well in combination with pumpkins, maize, squash and cucumbers, although they do inhibit the growth of some other plants. Potatoes planted close by will do especially badly.

MAINTENANCE

Seedlings are very tempting to slugs, so be vigilant. In addition ants seem to love nibbling away at the base of the stems. If you don't stop the ants in time the plant may fall over and die. At the first signs of ant interest I find that crushing a garlic clove or two and scattering around the base of the stem works as an effective deterrent. Rotate your sunflower patch around the garden to avoid disease such as Sclerotina rotting away the stems and flowerheads. Sunflowers may also occasionally suffer from downy mildew or rust.

Mulching your sunflowers well at the beginning of the growing season will help retain moisture in the soil, keeping your flowers stronger during dry periods. Mulching will also reduce competition from weeds. Tall varieties may require staking to prevent them falling, especially in exposed sites and windy conditions.

HARVESTING, PROCESSING AND STORAGE

Leaves are best collected before flowering and either used fresh or dried for later use.

Collect seeds in late summer when the back of the seedhead starts to turn a lemony colour and the seedheads hang a little, no longer following the path of the sun. Cut the whole head with a length of around 30cm of stem and hang upside down to dry. Either place a newspaper beneath to catch the falling seed or contain the head in a paper bag to keep it safe from hungry birds and mice. When the heads are completely dry, gently rub to release any remaining seeds. Store seed in a cool dry place in an airtight container. It is best to use them within a year. Due to the high vitamin E content the oil is pretty stable and stores well even when unrefrigerated. For maximum shelf life keep in a dark glass container and refrigerate.

USES

FOOD

The seeds are high in iron, calcium, fibre and vitamins B and E. To gain the maximum benefits eat the dehulled seeds raw. You can eat them by the handful, add them to salads, sprinkle over soups, make raw pâtés or add a handful to the blender to thicken up a smoothie. If you are looking for a healthy alternative to dairy products the seeds can be made into a seed milk or fermented and made into yoghurt or cheese. One hundred grams of seed contains 120mg of calcium which is marginally higher than cow's milk which contains 118mg[32] so you need not worry that you would be missing out on calcium. To make milk blend a handful of seed with a large glass of water and strain for the milk to be smooth or leave the seed remnants in for a thicker consistency. Experiment with the proportion of water to seed until you find your prefered consistency. To make yoghurt use 5 parts water to 4 parts seed, blend then leave the mixture in a glass jar covered with a cheesecloth or teatowel which will allow it to breathe. You will need to find a spot with a relatively stable temperature of between 21-37°C (70-100°F) for the fermentation process to take place. The higher the temperature, the quicker it will be ready - anything from 6-24 hours. Once it tastes rather tart and lemony and has bubbles showing on the surface your yoghurt is ready. The yoghurt will have risen as the bacteria which create it expel carbon dioxide. This is the main reason not to cover it with a tight fitting lid during the fermentation process. There will be a centimeter or

two of liquid at the bottom of your jar. This is whey and you may drink it if you choose or discard it. Once the fermentation process is complete cover with a screw cap and store in the fridge for up to a week. To make a soft cheese make sure all the whey has drained from your fresh yoghurt then pour onto cheesecloth and hang to air dry. Leave overnight and it will be ready for use by the morning. If you prefer a harder cheese, spread the fresh yoghurt on a non stick sheet and place in a dehydrator or the oven at a temperature of around 57°C (135°F). If spread thinly it will dry in around 6 hours and be brittle when done. A thickness of 1cm will take between 12-15 hours and remain a little chewy.

Lightly toasted seed, although not as nutritious as raw seed, have a great flavour and can be sprinkled over all kinds of dishes to give a tasty crunch. Seeds can also be added to baked goods including breads or thrown into soups and stews. Roasted, ground seed mixed with hot water makes a drink that some people choose instead of coffee.

Seeds can also be sprouted within a couple of days and have a really tangy taste. Simply soak overnight and then rinse once or twice daily until two large green leaves emerge. During the sprouting process all the minerals, vitamins and enzymes multiply in quantity, becoming more available and are thus more readily absorbed by the body. If you want some healthy greens in winter, sprinkle some seed over a tray of compost, lightly cover with a fine layer of compost, water regularly and watch them grow. Once your baby sunflowers have reached a height of about 8cm cut them and add to salads.

Cold press seeds to extract high quality oil. The oil is light with a neutral flavour so is good combined with stong flavoured herbs in salad dressings. Unlike many of the oils I have mentioned in this book sunflower is one that can withstand high temperatures and is therefore suitable for cooking. I would, however, caution against cooking with any oil regularly as it is difficult to digest and causes chemical alterations in the food which can become toxins in our bodies. If allowed to accumulate they will cause health problems over time. Make sure if you fry or roast foods in oil that you also eat plenty of raw green vegetables to help your body cleanse and expel toxins.

Petals can also be plucked and added raw to dishes to brighten up their colour, adding a slightly bitter yet sweet flavour. Young flower buds can also be eaten by preparing them in a similar way to globe artichokes.

Medicine

Eating a handful of seeds on a daily basis will give you plenty of vitamin E which is essential for circulatory health, will give your skin a healthy glow and will help guard against free radical damage, protecting your body from disease. In addition regular consumption of the seed will help lower cholesterol. Eating chlorophyll rich sprouted seeds regularly will have a cleansing effect on the liver and blood, giving a boost of energy whilst calming inflammations and reducing body odours.

A seed infusion will soothe coughs, whooping cough, bronchitis, bronchial infections and asthma. The vitamin E content will help reduce inflammation, easing arthritis and rheumatism. It will also relieve colds. A leaf infusion will make a potent remedy so only consume a maximum of 1 cup a day, a teaspoon at a time. This will treat diarrhoea, fevers and respiratory tract infections.

On an energetic level sunflower can help lift the spirits, boosting self esteem, promoting optimism and generally bringing the energy of a bright summer's day to any individual feeling a bit down or lacking confidence. It works on the solar plexus which is the location of the

3rd chakra. This area of the body energetically relates to self esteem and intuition. To receive these benefits just plant a few seeds, watch them grow and spend time amongst them, especially when they come into flower. Alternatively, make a flower essence which can be used throughout the year.

There are no known cautions or contraindications for using sunflower medicinally.

CLOTHING

Fibre collected from the stem can be used to make fine, soft clothes. First remove the soft pith then leave to ret (see flax p74 for method) before separating the fibres and spinning into yarn. You could try scutching the fibres which literally means scraping them out of the stem, but retting will facilitate the process by rotting away the unwanted plant matter, making it cleaner and easier to then spin into useable lengths.

FUEL

The dried stalks can be burned for heat generation and the remaining ash can be used as a fertiliser in the garden as the potassium levels remain high. Dried stalks and husks can also be used for kindling. The stalks can be fermented into cellulosic ethanol to fuel petrol engines and the oil can be added to diesel or used as it is

to run a diesel engine without any adjustments and allegedly without causing any damage.

GARDEN

The stalks and discarded hulls can be used as mulch.

The flowerheads attract bees, butterflies, birds, pest predators and other wildlife to the garden.

Sunflowers are great fun to grow as they grow so fast with such bright flowers and are perfect for encouraging young children into the garden and planting their first seeds.

MISCELLANEOUS

For a cheap and cheerful gift, grow some dwarf varieties in a pot and give freely. It cannot fail to make the recipient smile. Equally sunflowers make stunning cut flowers to liven up any living space when there is grey sky outside.

Use the flowers to produce a yellow dye and some seed varieties for a dark purple dye.

Birds including poultry love the seed and will peck them straight from the seed head but this could work against you if your local wild birds spot them before you harvest the flowerheads. It makes a good addition to winter seed mixes scattered outside to help wild birds through lean periods.

If you have crushed the seed to extract the oil, the remains (seedcake) can be fed to livestock, poultry, rabbits and pets such as hamsters and gerbils. Leaves and stalks can also be fed fresh to horses, cattle and sheep or made into silage.

Blend the oil with linseed and other ingredients in varnishes and paints.

The oil can be used as a lubricant for machinery.

Sunflower oil is nourishing to all, even oily, skin types. It will reduce the size of skin pores and makes a great base oil in which to infuse herbs when making preparations for eczema, psoriasis, acne, haemorrhoids, bruising and skin ulcers. It spreads well and is easily absorbed by the skin so can be used for massage. It feels softer when combined with fattier oils such as olive or sweet almond. Massaging with sunflower oil will stimulate circulation and improve the appearance of cellulite. Add a dash with some essential oils to bath water for an uplifting, skin nourishing experience.

The oil can be used as an ingredient in homemade soaps and candles.

Stalks and discarded hulls can be used as bedding for livestock.

Fibre from the inner stalk can be made into paper. The seed husks can also be pulped and made into a very absorbent paper that can be used for blotting ink.

As a point of interest the pith found in the centre of the stalk is much lighter than even cork and so has been used as the buoyant filling in life jackets and life belts. Further industrial uses of sunflower include its potential to clean up polluted water. This technique, called rhizofiltration, involves growing sunflowers hydroponically in vast mats and placing them directly on the affected water's surface. The extensive root network then reaches down, drawing up and extracting many pollutants including heavy metals that are present in the water. This method was used successfully in the former USSR after the Chenobyl nuclear disaster and is thought to have extracted up to 95% of the radioactivity that had leaked into the water.

NOTES

32. Steve Meyerowitz, *Kitchen Garden Cookbook* (Sproutman Publications, 1983), 89.

SWEET CHESTNUT
(Castanea sativa)

SWEET CHESTNUT IS often associated with love and is a food traditionally fed to a sweetheart. The nuts always take me back to childhood Christmases wandering along Oxford Street in London looking at the lights and nibbling on a bag of freshly roasted nuts. Even the people selling them intrigued me as they always seemed to be the warmest people around, standing next to their glowing orange coals.

This tree is not a native to the UK and, like so many other plants, was actually introduced by the Romans. On older trees you will often see the bark has a twisted pattern. This may be an indicator of ring shake within the trunk but makes for a rather attractive tree, even in the leafless months. If you are growing this tree for wood then you need to coppice it as the trunk in standard grown individuals is often afflicted with ring shake, making it unsuitable for most uses. Larger coppiced stems of sweet chestnut have a low sapwood content and less sapwood means that there is a higher proportion of the much more durable heartwood. The low sapwood content and natural durability of sweet chestnut, plus the ease with which it splits along the grain, make it a popular and versatile wood to work with. Splitting along the grain or 'cleaving' means the end product is stronger than a piece of wood that is sawn as the fibres remain intact.

The leaves give a wonderful autumn colour display through the full range of reds, crimsons, oranges and yellows. Don't confuse it with horse chestnut whose leaves are bigger and whose seed cases have short, bumpy spikes as opposed to fine and dense hair like spikes. The nut or conker inside the horse chestnut case is inedible and slightly toxic, so if foraging make sure you have the correct identification before you start eating.

The flowers make up one of the Bach flower remedies. This remedy is for people who have reached the limits of their endurance and are in a state of complete despair with no visible way out of their difficulties. Consuming the remedy helps restore a sense of hope and personal strength that allows you to forge onwards.

Varieties

There are around 10 species within the *Castanea* genus. Most common is *Castanea sativa.* Marron de Lyon is one named variety that will fruit in just 5 years.

In trials the cultivars Marigoule and Vignols have both produced over 40kg of nuts per tree on specimens that were only 10 years old[33].

Growth Habits

Sweet chestnut prefers sandy or silty soil with a rather acidic pH of around 4.0-4.5. Sweet chestnut is native to warmer climates than you generally find in the UK so avoid planting in a frost pocket, aim for a more sheltered location. They can survive the salty spray of maritime conditions but will not fruit as well in such locations. Nuts grown in the UK will generally be smaller than ones you can buy as these will have been produced in more optimum conditions with hotter summers. Trees grown in the south where temperatures remain a little warmer will have a higher nut yield than trees grown in the north, at high elevations or in exposed conditions.

Being a woodland tree a little shade is not a problem. Once established they can cope with drought conditions. New growth is sensitive to late frosts which will affect the years nut production, luckily chestnut doesn't tend to flower until June so in all but the most exposed locations your nuts should be safe. They are poor self pollinators so unless you have another sweet chestnut growing locally it would be advisable to plant two of them. If growing in an orchard give the trees an 8 to 12m spacing.

In optimum conditions and

when grown primarily for the nuts sweet chestnut can achieve a height of up to 35m and a diameter of up to 2m. With age older, higher branches tend to break off, losing some of the height as a result. Sweet chestnut makes a great companion for pine trees as it will neutalise some of the added acidity that falling pine needles will impart to the soil beneath. Chestnuts also grow well in the vicinity of oaks.

Nuts may not be produced every year especially in colder climates and sometimes only yield well at intervals of up to 4 years. Luckily they are not as palatable to squirrels as some nuts, however when ripe and fallen to the floor they are a tempting treat for deer, so if you have a high population in your area you need to be out there quick to get the harvest for yourself. They take between 7-10 years to start producing nuts and will be at peak production as early as 12 years after planting. After 60 years the nut harvest will gradually begin to decline. During the years of peak productivity you can expect a harvest of anything between 30kg to over 100kg depending on variety, siting and microclimate[34]. If you are after the wood then coppice in cycles of 10-16 years.

New trees can be easily grown from fresh nuts sown in late autumn. They will usually germinate in late winter or early spring. It is advisable to protect them in a cold frame for their first couple of winters. Once the tree has reached a height of between 20 and 40cm it is ready to plant out in the place you would like it to grow.

MAINTENANCE

Grey squirrels sometimes strip the bark. If you find this to be a problem you will have to find a way of removing the squirrels.

Place a layer of good quality compost around the base of the tree every couple of years to keep it in peak condition as it has high nutrient requirements.

HARVESTING, PROCESSING AND STORAGE

The nuts are formed within a prickly case and will fall to the ground when ripe. This tends to coincide with the leaves falling, usually from October onwards, although start checking from September. Each case contains two or three nuts and will open to release the nuts when they are ripe. Once they are on the ground collect quickly or they will begin to deteriorate. If you live in an area of extreme winters and heavy snows have been predicted you will need to pick the nuts from the tree before they fall as severe cold will make them taste bitter. If collecting from the tree don't pluck off the prickly cases but take a knife and prise them open as plucking the cases directly from the tree will affect next year's harvest. Before storing be sure to check all the nuts for holes or cracks and discard any damaged ones. Hang them in an onion bag so that air can circulate. If they get damp they will go mouldy and mould spreads through them quickly, so check your store regularly.

Collect leaves in June or July for medicinal purposes and use fresh or dry for later use.

USES

FOOD

The nuts are delicious roasted over hot coals but split the shell with a knife first or they have a tendancy to explode! You can also eat them raw, although they are harder to peel this way.

The nuts can be ground into a gluten free flour which is commonly used in rural chestnut growing areas of France and Italy. The flour can be used to make pancakes and cookies but as it lacks gluten the finished products are somewhat crumbly. Chopped nuts are often used in stuffing recipes and for making purées and soups. The nuts are carbohydrate rich and a good source of fatty acids and protein.

Beer can be brewed from the starch of the nut as is done on the French island of Corsica.

MEDICINE

The leaves are used medicinally. They are astringent and also help relieve coughs. An infusion of the leaves will bring relief to spasmodic and even severe coughs such as whooping cough. In addition they will help to dry up diarrhoea and heavy menstrual bleeding. The infusion is rather strong so only consume a maximum of three tablespoons four times a day. Using the infusion as a gargle will bring some relief to sore throats and pharyngitis.

There are no reported cautions or contraindications for using sweet chestnut leaves medicinally.

FUEL

The wood can be burned although it is best in a woodburner as it tends to spit. It takes a long time to season fully - around 24 months - so it would not be the first choice to grow as a fuel wood. It can also be used to make good quality charcoal.

BUILDING AND HOUSING

Planks are great to use for cladding, decking and floor boards. Sweet chestnut wood is especially durable and so once in place requires very little maintenance or surface treatment. Thin strips can be split off, known as laths. These can be woven into a lattice or nailed in rows to a framing support which can then be used as a substructure for plaster work or roofing where slates, shingles or tiles can be laid. Lattice work for the walls of yurts and roof poles can also be made from sweet chestnut.

Shingles for roofing can be made from sweet chestnut. The colour will grey naturally with time but they last well and look great on a naturally built house.

Sweet chestnut wood can be used for wooden frames in buildings and window frames. Using roundwood is much more energy efficient and provides a stronger frame than sawn wood. You will save money and time if you are not milling your wood into planks whilst at the same time you will be maintaining the structuaral integrity of the tree. You can roughly square the outside edges with a hand tool such as an adze. Some old wooden buildings built using roundwood poles are still in existence 1000 years after construction, so if done well you may end up with a wonderfully enduring structure.

HOUSEHOLD

The coppiced wood can be used in turnery and furniture making.

GARDEN

The wood is naturally rot resistant and so is great for making all kinds of outdoor items and structures such as picnic tables, benches, bird tables, bird boxes, gates and hurdles. You can also create attractive lattice work structures for supporting climbing plants, for example arches, pergolas, trellis work and arbours. Due to the strength and durability of chestnut it is a perfect wood for making fences and stakes, especially if made from cleft wood as this will be stonger still. An untreated chestnut stake will last up to 25 years in the ground before it needs to be replaced.

When cutting wood into planks a byproduct is slab, the outer curved section of wood with the bark attached. Slab is a great edging material for raised beds and chestnut slab is especially enduring. Other outdoor projects can also be constructed from slab wood. We had a rustic summer house made from slab in the garden of my childhood home.

The leaves rot slowly and so can be used in the garden where needed as a weed supressing mulch.

20 AMAZING PLANTS

Alternatively the leaves can be collected up in autumn, stored in a black bag and given a generous watering and in two years you will find perfectly rotted and nutrient rich leaf mould to spread over your vegetable beds.

The flowers, which bloom in July, attract wildlife and provide an excellent source of nectar for bees, who in turn pollinate them.

MISCELLANEOUS

Sweet chestnut makes a good walking stick.

From the laths you can make rustic trugs for collecting your produce.

The logs can be inoculated with mushroom spores so that you can grow your own mushrooms (see p183).

A shampoo can be made from an infusion of the leaves and the skins of the nuts which contain saponins (see nettle p140 for method). It will give a lovely gloss and good condition to your hair.

NOTES

33. Martin Crawford "*A.R.T. 2006 Trial Ground Report*" Agroforestry News Volume 15, Number 2, February 2007, 3.

34. Patrick Whitefield, *The Earth Care Manual* (Permanent Publications, 2004), 223.

WALNUT
(Juglans regia)

THE LATIN *JULGLANS* derives from Jupiter glans which means Jupiter's acorn or literally a nut fit for a god. This tree is native to the Balkans in south eastern Europe and the north west Himalayas. In some cultures the nuts symbolise fertility and were at one time thrown at weddings, although I think I prefer the idea of rose petals or hops! If you receive a bag of walnuts it is said that you will see all your wishes fulfilled, so I say we should all plant a tree and generously give bags of nuts to all our friends and neighbours!

The dense, fine grained timber can range in colour from honey to a very dark chocolatey brown. The grain can be straight but may also appear in sweeping curves, waves and sunburst patterns. The wood is lightweight, shock-resistant, hard, strong, durable and flexible. The wood does not warp, shrink or splinter. The shock resistant properties of walnut make it ideal for gun and pistol stocks and as a result the walnut population was decimated during the time of the Napoleonic wars when many guns and pistols were being produced. Unfortunately it was never replanted in the quantities that it had previously enjoyed. The most valuable timber lies at the root crown where you will find beautiful patterns and swirls in the wood. To access this sought after decorative wood does, however, mean totally uprooting the tree.

VARIETIES

There are 21 species within the genus *Juglans* but I shall concentrate on *Juglans regia,* also known as Persian, English or common walnut.

Juglans nigra, or black walnut, found in North America is grown mainly for its good quality timber and medicinal qualities which do vary from those of the common walnut. The nuts themselves are much smaller with a thicker shell than the common walnut, hence the reason they are rarely grown for the nut and more commonly for their straight timber.

There are a selection of hybrid cultivars that have been bred to have a heavy crop or to be more frost resistant and in addition to crop at an age of only 3-4 years. Some popular cultivars are:

Buccaneer which gives a heavy nut crop.

Corne du Perigord, a late leaf, disease resistant heavy cropper.

Fernor and Fernette, both reliable croppers in the UK climate, being late leafing and disease resistant.

Franquette which is late leafing and disease resistant but slow to come into fruiting (taking up to 15 years to get a decent crop), however worth the wait as the nuts are large and tasty.

Rita has a heavy yield of nuts from a young age.

GROWTH HABITS

Walnuts thrive during warm summers and are susceptible to damage by both early and late frosts, so plant in a sheltered spot. Late frosts can take out fresh shoots and flowers and even kill a young tree. It is therefore worth protecting seedlings, especially over their first winters. A healthy walnut will on average reach a height of around 18m, although heights of 30m are not unknown. The length of trunk below the first branches is short while the spread of the branches is wide, approximating the height. Walnut is self-fertile and wind pollinated but will produce more and bigger nuts if cross pollinated with another tree. If growing in an orchard setting a spacing of 8 to 15m between walnuts is recommended. It will need full sun for the nuts to fully ripen. It will survive well on most soils but absolutely thrives in deep, rich, well drained soils. Walnut will not endure waterlogging.

The roots secrete a substance called juglone which has an inhibitory effect on the growth of many other species. It is the walnut's defence mechanism, protecting itself from other plants that would be competing for resources if they grew too close. The influence of the juglone extends at least as far as the spread of the canopy. Rain dripping off the leaves, falling leaves and nuts also have an inhibitory effect on other plant life. Juglone stays in the soil for a number of years after the tree has been removed, making it difficult to replant that spot with juglone sensitive species, which ironically include walnut, for some time. This effect is much reduced in common walnut as opposed to black walnut but it is still worth planting sensitive species such as apple, birch, tomatoes and potatoes with caution. Grasses will, however, survive under the dense, shady canopy so it could be a worthy tree to dot around dedicated pasture or at the back of a lawn. Cereals and some fruit trees such as pear and plum are successfully grown around walnuts, making your list of options for a polyculture wider.

New trees are easily propagated by placing a fresh nut in good quality moist compost. Walnuts start producing good yields after 6-10 years and can enjoy good productivity for over 100 years. Walnut is usually cropped for timber at around 60 years which is before the quality of the timber starts to decline. This still leaves many years of nut production before harvesting the wood.

They should produce nuts every year once they get going and depending on variety can produce from 7.5 to 15 tonnes per hectare at peak productivity[35]. It can take up to 20 years to reach peak productivity, although the newer varieties will mature earlier, perhaps after only 15 years. To put this in an easier to envisage format you can expect to produce around 5kg per tree each year at the beginning of its productivity and up to about 75kg each year at its peak[36]. Grafted saplings, like many of the cultivars, will produce nuts much sooner than a regular common walnut grown from seed.

MAINTENANCE

Once established walnut requires very little maintenance, just the removal of any damaged or dead wood to maintain the vitality of the rest of the tree. If you are growing for both nuts and timber, prune the stem, only allowing the first branches to emerge at a height of 2.4m. This will give good quality knot free timber and still produce an abundance of nuts. Any pruning is best undertaken in late autumn after the last leaves have fallen. It is perhaps worth knowing that any damage sustained by the bark may result in the production of burred grain in the timber, highly prized by craftsmen for its beautiful patterning.

To improve the nut yield it is worth laying some good quality compost around the base every few years as walnut has high nutrient requirements.

Blight can be a problem if cool, wet weather is experienced during flowering. The only real way of avoiding this is to seek out blight resistant varieties.

HARVESTING, PROCESSING AND STORAGE

Collect the green husks from July onwards. They will stain your fingers a tobacco orange colour but this is not permanent. If you wish to avoid it wear gloves whilst handling them. Collect the nuts as they ripen from late October through November. Dehusked nuts with intact shells will store for a year or more in a cool, dry place and keeping them in a box of salt or sand will extend their storage time. Leaves can be collected throughout the growing season and either dried for later use or used fresh.

USES

FOOD

Nuts can be harvested early, in June or July before the shells have formed. The nuts will still be green and wet and cannot be eaten raw but may be pickled and are considered a delicacy. Cover with boiling water and rub off any fuzz from the surface of the nuts then boil until the water is dark. Pour off the water and repeat until the water remains clear. Place the walnuts in a jar with salt, ginger, black pepper, bay leaves, mustard seeds, horseradish, lemon slices, cloves, mace and a few walnut leaves. Cover with boiling vinegar and seal the jar. Leave for at least 30 days to pickle before eating[37]. Alternatively add 150g of sugar to half a bottle of gin, top up with green walnuts and shake regularly for a couple of months before tasting your own home made walnut liqueur!

Ripe nuts collected in the autumn have a rich flavour which intensifies as they dry. I prefer to eat them fresh from the tree when the flavour is more subtle and the texture more moist and fleshy than the brittleness they assume on drying. Once dried they can still be eaten raw, crumbled and added to salads, used in place of pinenuts in pesto and in all manner of sweet and savoury dishes, from cakes to lasagne. They are rich in protein, containing the same quantity per gram as chicken. They also contain potassium, magnesium, phosphorus, iron, calcium, zinc, copper and vitamins A, B complex and E making them a nutritious addition to the diet. The nuts can also be ground into a flour and added to fruit cakes and nut breads.

The nuts can be cold pressed to extract a delicious, yellow coloured oil that is high in health giving omega 3s (ALAs). It has a very distinctive flavour and to benefit most from this it should always be consumed raw, either in salad dressings or drizzled over soups, risottos and other hot dishes that have been plated up and are ready to be served. Always store in a dark glass container in the fridge as when stored in this way it should remain good for anything between 6-24 months. Once it has reached 6 months in age smell before using to check for rancidity.

The sap can be tapped in spring (see birch p62 for methodology) to get a sugary liquid that you can simply drink as it comes or concentrate through evaporation into a sticky syrup.

The leaves can be used to wrap fresh home made cheeses to which they will impart a subtle flavour.

MEDICINE

A decoction made from the husks will treat diarrhoea and anaemia and adding a teaspoon of honey and gargling with it will soothe and treat sore throats. Husks can also be made into a salve for irritated skin, minor burns, dry eczema and wounds.

Drink an infusion made from the leaves for chronic coughs, asthma, constipation and to restore vigour after a lengthy illness. The infusion will also help dissolve both kidney and urinary stones. It will ease inflammatory skin conditions including acne and psoriasis and can be used externally as a skin wash to improve eczema and herpes. Use as a mouthwash for mouth sores and ulcers. Dried, ground leaves can be applied to moist skin conditions such as weeping eczema and flesh wounds and will help dry them up whilst guarding against infection and reducing inflammation.

The cold pressed oil can be applied to both skin and nails to help improve circulation, heal skin ulcers and improve the condition of brittle nails. It can also be used as the base for infused oil preparations made for the treatment of acne, eczema and itchy, inflamed skin. The oil can be massaged into the scalp to soothe an itchy, flaky scalp and reduce dandruff. Leave it on for a couple of hours before rinsing off with a mild shampoo and repeat 2 or 3 times a week until the itchiness has gone. It can be used alone or infused with St John's wort to soothe and heal minor burns and sunburn.

Simply eating a few nuts a day will help lower LDLs while increasing HDLs, improving overall cardiovascular health.

There are no reported cautions or contraindications for using walnut medicinally.

Fuel

The wood can be cut into logs and used as fuel, although this would only really be applicable to rotten wood or thin branches that could not be put to other use due to the high value of the timber. It will spit and snap as it burns so is probably best for use inside a woodburner rather than an open fire, although it is very fragrant when it burns. It does put out a lot of heat, burning at high temperatures, but must be seasoned first for at least a year.

Household

Walnut wood has a beautiful grain and pattern and so is desirable for making furniture such as chairs and tables or using as a veneer on household furnishings. The timber can be used for solid wood work surfaces, bespoke kitchen units, cabinet making and shelving.

The long, straight lengths of timber can make attractive and hard wearing floorboards. Commercially you are more likely to find floor boards made from black walnut, although common walnut can also provide the timber for good quality hard wearing boards.

The nut oil can be applied directly as a wood polish. If you have no way of pressing the oil simply crush a nut and rub it over your wooden surface. As the natural oils are released gently work them into the wood by rubbing the nut pulp over the surface. When you are done wipe clean with a cloth and you will see a rich and luxuriant sheen to your newly moisturised piece of wood. For a more durable finish, useful for wooden surfaces that get a lot of use, try mixing walnut oil with beeswax. Gently heat the walnut oil, adding beeswax gradually, either grated from a block or using pellets. Continue until you have added twice the weight of wax to the weight of oil. During this process do not allow it to boil and keep on a low heat, constantly adding more wax and stirring as it melts. You should end up with a similar consistency to a salve or balm. Check the consistency by dripping a little onto a plate and leaving it for a few seconds to harden. It should yield to the warmth of your finger relatively easily. If it is too hard just add a little more oil or if too soft add a little more wax. Pour into a wide necked screw top jar and allow to cool thoroughly before putting the lid on. This mixture will store for several years. If it gets too hard whilst in storage just leave it out in the sun for a day and it will soften a little. To use apply to the wooden surface with a rag, leave for a couple of hours and reapply. After a couple more hours take a clean cloth and wipe the woodwork down, removing any excess wax and oil. I find the whole process meditative and find myself really appreciating the beautiful grain of the wood I am working on.

Garden

Old crushed up shells can be used as a slow rotting mulch.

Miscellaneous

Make a natural hair rinse for dying your hair dark brown or black. First make a tincture (see p179) from the green husks, perfume with a little essential oil and simply rub into the hair after washing. If you have no access to walnut husks you can use nuts. Crush a handful and leave to infuse in cold water for four days then strain. Work the liquid into your hair with your hands, cover with a plastic bag and leave for 30 minutes then rinse off before shampooing. Beware! Either liquid will stain everything black so wear old clothes, plastic gloves and protect any surfaces, including the floor. You may even want to run a line of petroleum jelly around your hairline to

prevent any drips coming into contact with your skin and staining your face or neck.

The husks, bark, leaf and shell of walnut can all be used to dye fabrics. Each part gives a different colour so test with just a swatch of fabric first to check the shade. As with all natural dyes the colour will vary from batch to batch. The bark will give a soft, brown dye while the green husks will give a yellow colour.

Leaves and husks when crushed and rubbed over the skin will act as an insect repellent. If applying to the skin always patch test first in case of sensitivity. An infusion of the leaves left to cool and then thoroughly rubbed into animal fur will kill off fleas and lice. Leave the infusion to dry then brush well.

Bowls and goblets can be made by turning walnut wood. The finished pieces will be beautiful due to the unique patterns inherent within the wood and the natural shine that will occur without treatment or polishing.

If you have enough land to grow walnut for timber and have some mature trees ready for harvest it is worth bearing in mind that walnut, whether sawn for timber or veneer grade, will normally achieve at least double the price you would expect for oak. It will, however, vary considerably between trees depending on the size, quality and patterning of the timber.

Small sections of bark can be rubbed over the teeth and gums or chewed. The bark has an antibacterial action which in tests has proven beneficial in the prevention of dental caries, plaque and gum disease.

Pigment can be suspended in walnut oil to form a natural oil paint.

The oil can be used as an ingredient in home made soaps.

The oil has a dry nature and is easily absorbed into the skin, leaving it feeling soft and supple with no greasy residue. It is especially nourishing for mature skin types, being incredibly toning for elderly and sagging skin and excellent for skin regeneration. It contains GLAs which have an anti-inflammatory action and so it's also good to use on allergic and sensitive skin. Use on oily and large pored skin or blend with other oils such as pumpkin and evening primrose for use as an anti-wrinkle treatment. It is absorbed too quickly to be used alone as a massage oil. You would need to blend it with longer, fattier oils such as avocado or sweet almond first. It has a natural level of UV protection but do not use it alone as a sunscreen.

NOTES

35. Patrick Whitefield, *Woodland in Permaculture* (Patrick Whitefield, 1992), 39.

36. Patrick Whitefield, *The Earth Care Manual* (Permanent Publications, 2004), 223.

37. Ellen Evert Hopman, *Tree Medicine, Tree Magic* (Phoenix Publishing Inc., 1991), 144.

Willow baskets made by Norah Kennedy.

WILLOW
(Salix spp.)

WILLOW HAS A watery, flowing, flexible nature and a feminine feel to it. Willow has often been asociated with letting go and surrendering to the emotions, helping tears and grief pass and assisting the process of moving on and starting afresh. It has also had a long association with magic, willow being a prefered wood to use as a wand.

Willow provides light, soft timber. The thin rods or whips are extremely pliable when fresh and so bend particularly well without breaking. The rods that grow from the coppice stools are usually very straight. Stem colour varies widely between varieties but tends to fade after a couple of years' growth, so if you want a particular shade you must harvest the whips whilst they are young.

Willow is often pollarded as opposed to being coppiced, although in essence the two processes amount to the same thing. Wood is harvested from pollards in the winter but at a much greater height above the ground than coppice, usually between 1.8-3m. This prevents grazing animals nibbling away the newly growing shoots that will emerge in spring. The rods harvested from pollards are most often of a small diameter and used in basketry. Pollarding requires much more effort than regular coppicing as you will need a ladder and good balance to be able to harvest your underwood, so unless deer, grazing livestock or rampant rabbits cannot be kept away you would definitely be better off coppicing willow.

Varieties

There are around 400 *Salix* species and here are a few of the most common ones:

Bay willow *(Salix pentandra)* has both a height and spread of around 10m.

Common osier *(Salix viminalis)* is the most common species used for basketry and provides fast growing long stems. It reaches a height of 6m and a spread of 4m.

Crack Willow *(Salix fragilis)* can achieve a height and spread of up to 15m with a tolerance for less fertile soils.

Goat/pussy willow *(Salix caprea)* blossom appears in March, providing valuable early forage for bees.

Violet willow *(Salix daphnoides)* has mauve stems and will grow well in poor soil, prefering neutral or alkaline conditions. It can reach a height of 10m with a spread of 8m and a potential growth rate of 2m per year.

Weeping willow *(Salix babylonica)* grows to a height of 12m with a trunk diameter of 60cm. This to me is the classic willow and often found on the banks of a river or pond

looking feminine and majestic.

White willow *(Salix alba)* can grow to a height of 25m with a spread of 10m.

Salix glabra and *Salix nigricans* both have black stems.

Salix tortuosa remains quite small and has either red or yellow stems and *Salix erithroflexuosa* is a vigourous grower and green stemmed. Both have a curled habit to the stems, making them less useful but very beautiful.

Growth Habits

Willow is the fastest growing tree in the British climate, gaining up to 3.5m a year. Consequently the rotation time for willow coppice is very short, each tree being cut back to the stump every year or two. Willows produce catkins in spring which are pollinated by insects, providing a valuable source of nectar for bees early in the year. The seeds are wind distributed. One great advantage of willow is that a stem pushed cut side down into the earth will grow, making willow very easy to propagate and negating the need to nurture nursery trees. In fact this is the preferable way to grow willows as they do not tolerate root disturbance well. To ensure success plant the willow when dormant between November and March. Make sure the rod you are planting is around one or two years old and freshly cut with a diagonal cut at the end which is to be pushed into the ground. It also needs to be around 30cm long, two thirds of which should end up under ground level. Up to 50 cuttings can be planted in a 4 x 4m plot if growing for craft uses. If growing for fuel wood give each cutting a spacing of 1m² and for hedging leave 50cm between cuttings. Surround the cuttings with a good layer of mulch to supress weeds.

Willow prefers a sunny spot with moist, fertile soil. It acts as a pioneer species in damp, boggy areas, once established gradually modifying the environment to one more suitable for other plants to follow. It can tolerate wet and heavy soils and loves the fertile gloop that runs through sewers, so should be planted well away or the roots may attempt a break and entry for such fetid treasure. This feature can however be taken advantage of by planting it around a basic composting or long drop toilet and in such a location they will thrive on the nutrients and clean up any unsavoury run off. The robust root systems make it unwise to plant willow within 12m of buildings otherwise they may damage the foundations.

MAINTENANCE

They should be pruned around February time. The prunings are also most often part of your harvest and the thin rods also known as whips have a multitude of uses.

Mulching around your young trees is important as this will not only keep competitive weeds at bay but will also help to conserve essential moisture. As they love fertility it is a good idea to give them a feed of rich compost or other natural and organic fertiliser each year before putting down the mulch layer.

Willow will not survive in particularly dry conditions so if you have a long dry spell, especially in the early years, water regularly.

Some modern hybrids are particularly susceptible to fungal infections, especially rust but resistant varieties are becoming available. Rabbits can also cause an annoyance as they love to nibble on the tender shoots. A rabbit proof fence will be necessary if they are abundant in your area.

HARVESTING, PROCESSING AND STORAGE

Whips and thinner rods are harvested in winter after the leaves have dropped and the frosts have begun. Usually starting in November the harvest may continue into February. Stems only one year old called 'withies' are harvested for basket production. If you are intending to use your willow for living sculpture it is advisable to leave them attached to the coppice stump until they are going to be used. When freshly cut the whips and withies are naturally very pliable. They can be stored but if you do so you will need to soak them before use to restore their flexibility. If you have harvested whips for living sculpture before they are to be used they will need to be stored away from winds and direct sunlight standing upright with the cut end in water. It is important that they do not dry out or they will die.

Harvest sections of the bark for medicinal use in spring and throughout the summer, being careful to only take small sections and never a complete ring circling the trunk as this will kill the tree. Dry away from direct sunlight and store in as large a piece as possible to stall the oxidation process which otherwise breaks down the active ingredients, reducing the potency of the medicine. Crush or powder the bark just before use.

USES

MEDICINE

The bark of willow is where the medicine lies and although many species of willow can be used medicinally white willow (Salix alba) is the one that is most commonly used in any commercial preparations. The bark contains salicin which is converted in the stomach to salicylic acid, an anti-inflammatory that is also the active ingredient in the drug aspirin. In addition to being anti-inflammatory willow is also astringent, provides pain relief and helps reduce fever. A tincture or a decoction can be made from the bark and used to bring relief to muscular and joint pains including arthritis. It will help sweat out fevers during colds and bouts of the flu, provide pain relief from gout, rheumatism, backache, neuralgia, headaches and painful menstruation. When using a decoction you only need very small amounts, just one cupful throughout the day, a teaspoon at a time. You can also wash skin wounds such as minor burns and sores with the decoction and gargle with it for sore throats and gums.

Avoid using willow internally if you are pregnant, breast feeding or sensitive to aspirin.

FUEL

The fluffy seeds of goat willow (Salix caprea) can be used when starting a fire as they burn easily and well.

Willow coppiced in 3-4 year cycles can be chipped and burnt. A 5 year cycle will produce logs with a diameter of around 8cm. It burns at high temperatures and leaves little ash. I have seen willow faggots slipped into large ceramic woodburners where a single faggot seemed to last quite some time and put out considerable heat. Yields of 12-15 t/ha/ann dry weight can be expected on a 3 year rotation[38]. A quarter of an acre of short rotation willow coppice would be enough to keep a small, well insulated home heated using an efficient burner[39]. The wood has a high water content, meaning that seasoning is essential, and once seasoned your large, bulky bundles end up being pretty light. During burning it may spark so always be sure to use a fire guard or use in a woodburner.

BUILDING AND HOUSING

Thatching spars can be made from both crack and white willow that has been harvested on a 3 year rotation.

HOUSEHOLD

Woven items of furniture such as chairs and coffee tables can be made from willow.

GARDEN

Different outdoor structures can be woven from living willow. There are many different ways to weave living willow and a good place to start is with diagonal interlacing. This is a simple open weave that looks like regular link fencing creating diamond shapes. Lightly scratch back the outer layer of bark at the points where the rods cross and lash with willow or twine. The reason for using a diagonal weave is that the new growth will then occur all along the length of the stem as opposed to just at the top ends as it would if placed in an upright position. Once the new growth has reached a reasonable length it can be woven into the existing structure, giving it a thicker cover of foliage and a more sturdy appearance. Stems that are tightly lashed together will fuse over the course of little more than a year, growing into one cross shaped piece. Adding upright poles at spacings of around 25cm will create a stronger, more windproof structure. Don't forget to push a good 20cm of the rods that are in contact with the ground into the earth to ensure they set root and that your structure becomes a living one. Arches, bowers, tunnels and domes can all be created with living willlow.

Planted along the contours of unstable slopes and along the banks of streams and rivers willow's aggressively growing root systems can be employed to help stabilise soils, providing erosion control. They can also be planted as a hedge to create effective shelter belts or alongside reeds as functional parts of waste water cleaning systems.

If you have a large pond or lake on your land and want to increase your edges (the areas where the greatest biodiversity exists), provide sheltered habitats for ducks and other water fowl, or just generally increase your available growing area. Then you could attempt to create a version of the ancient Mesoamerican floating island system called chinampas, originally employed by the Aztecs who constructed these stationary yet floating islands from a lattice of canes covered with earth and edged with willow. I have seen a version where fingers are extended from the shoreline into the waterbody. Make them from locally avaliable materials such as cut reeds and mud then edge with willow stakes which when they take root serve to secure the edges.

Harvested rods can be woven into hurdles, plant supports, plant protectors (to keep grazing livestock out) and fences which create great wind breaks, slowing the wind yet letting some pass through.

An extract made from willow can be used as a rooting hormone when you are propagating plants with cuttings. All salix varieties contain indolebutyric acid (IBA), a naturally occuring chemical that is a plant growth regulator. Collect a handful of pencil sized fresh willow twigs, chop into sections 5-10cm long, place in a pan and cover with boiling water. Use half a measuring cup of twigs for every litre of water. Leave the twigs to infuse in the water overnight then strain. The liquid can be stored in the fridge for up to two months. Keep in sealed containers and be sure to label with both the contents and the date made. Each time you do a cutting soak the base (or cut part of the leaf) in a little of the liquid overnight before planting and the IBA will be absorbed into the stem (or leaf), encouraging root growth whilst inhibiting fungal, bacterial and viral disease.

Willow plays host to a huge number of fauna, supporting the diversity of local ecosystems.

MISCELLANEOUS

Thin rods and withies are exceptionally pliable and perfect for basket making. Leave them outside for a few weeks after harvesting to 'weather' before use. With practice all sizes and shapes of basket can be produced, from laundry baskets to coffins for green funerals.

Rods can be made into charcoal for use by artists.

Withies can be used like twine to tie bundles.

The boiled roots of crack

willow produce a purple dye.

If you are feeling creative and are short of footwear willow is the traditional wood used for Dutch clogs! They never look that comfy to me but at least made from willow they are light on the foot.

Cricket bats are traditionally made from willow.

Catkins look great in a bunch of spring cut flowers to brighten up your home.

A leaf infusion or bark decoction can be used as a rinse on clean hair to treat dandruff.

Fibres found in the inner bark of crack and white willow can be used to make flexible cordage, while the bark from pussy willow can be used to make rope.

To make paper from the stems of black willow (*Salix nigra*) harvest in spring or summer and strip the leaves. Steam the stems until the fibres peel off then cook the fibres with lye or wood ash for a further 2 hours. Rinse thoroughly before beating or blending the remains and putting in a paper frame to dry. The paper will be a reddish brown colour.

NOTES

38. Patrick Whitefield, *Woodland in Permaculture* (Patrick Whitefield, 1992), 38.

39. Patrick Whitefield "*Thinking Globally Acting Locally*" Permaculture No.65, Autumn 2010, 24.

PLANT-BASED FUELS: TOWARDS A GREENER FUTURE?

Plant based fuels, known as biofuels, are made from biomass as opposed to fossilised material (which forms petrol, diesel, natural gas and coal). Part of the reason that biofuels have been touted as a green solution is that plants absorb CO_2 as they grow, thus reducing the overall impact when they are burned and making them more or less carbon neutral. However, as with most things, once crops are produced on a commercial scale to provide fuel they are grown conventionally with large quantities of fossil fuel based fertilisers and pesticides causing an overall increase in the amount of CO_2 being produced. In addition mass produced biofuel crops tend to be grown on land that has previously been forest or used for growing food, causing much controversy and debate. Some crops are worse offenders than others: palm oil for example is deemed especially bad because huge areas of ancient forest with a large diversity of species and an abundance of natural resources are being felled to make way for huge palm oil monocultures. Despite this biofuels cannot be discounted as a bad thing, especially if the plant material used for fuel production is, for example, a by-product of another crop. A major benefit

of using biofuels besides the obvious environmental ones (biomass being biodegradable, less polluting and entirely renewable) is that using biofuels provides much greater energy security than using finite fossil fuels.

For each plant included in the directory I have mentioned their individual potential fuel uses, and in addition Appendix II (p179) gives greater detail on fuel wood and charcoal production and use. So in this chapter I am merely providing a brief overview of the ways biomass can be used to provide fuels for running engines. This can be done individually on a small scale or as part of a fuel producing co-op. Fuel producing co-ops are becoming more popular and are a way of sharing resources and knowledge with the added bonus of friendly support. If there is not already one in your area gather some willing friends and form one of your own.

SVOs

Straight vegetable oils (SVOs) are made from pressing the oil from seeds. They can be used in a diesel engine but are much more viscous than petroleum diesel and so your engine would require a little modification before use. SVOs are particularly susceptible to cold so over winter you will need to blend them with petroleum diesel. The colder it is the higher proportion of petroleum diesel you will need. A more radical approach is to fit an SVO conversion into your engine which preheats the oil, allowing it to run even in cold conditions.

Diesel engines were originally made to run on SVOs and in fact when Rudolph Diesel demonstrated his first diesel engine it was fueled with peanut oil and he considered hemp oil an ideal fuel. Diesel engines have evolved from their early design, however, and newer fuel-injection engines may react badly to simply slinging in some vegetable oil. Still some oils, such as sunflower, can be used untreated. There are many online forums debating how much straight oil is OK to use and which engines take them better. If you are serious about giving it a try I would recommend doing some online research so that you can make a well informed decision before giving it a go. The best general advice it seems at this point is to add 20% sunflower oil (or other 'vegetable' oil such as rapeseed) to your petroleum diesel and increase incrementally if it seems there is no compromise to performance.

As SVOs are generally too viscous to use in modern diesel engines, if you want to avoid blending with petroleum diesel the alternative is to convert the SVO into biodiesel by the process of transesterification.

BIODIESEL

Transesterification combines the SVO with a methoxide catalyst and the result is the separation of the oil into usable fuel oil and a glycerol by-product. It may sound complex but I have been assured it is a relatively simple process. Once processed biodiesel will burn up to 75% cleaner than petroleum diesel, producing 80% less CO_2 and no sulphur. In addition it is 98% biodegradable in just 21 days[40]. It can be used directly in any existing diesel engine either alone or mixed in any ratio with petroleum diesel. In commercial blends the quantity of biodiesel is usually between 5-20%. A side benefit is that the by-product glycerol can be used in soaps and other products.

Biodiesel is an incredible solvent and cleaning agent which will have side effects on your diesel engine as it will slowly but surely dissolve paints and rubber. Until 1993 fuel lines in most vehicles were made from rubber which will slowly disintegrate over time if you are using biodiesel. The disintegration will occur more rapidly the higher the proportion of biodiesel you are using. The simple solution is to replace any rubber fuel lines with biodiesel compatible ones. Biodiesel will also dissolve and move old fuel deposits in your fuel delivery system, eventually clogging your fuel filter and at this point you will need to replace your filter. You will know when it has clogged as the accelerator response will feel slower than usual. Biodiesel does, however, run much cleaner than mineral diesel, so once you have been using it for a while the filter will be less likely to clog. Biodiesel is highly lubricating, reducing wear and tear on engine parts and actually extending the life of the engine. It does not work so well in cold temperatures so when it gets to freezing point outside you will need to blend it with petroleum diesel to keep your motor running smoothly. Other than that performance of biodiesel should be no different to that of regular petroleum diesel.

Biodiesel can also be obtained by processing old cooking oil, thereby reusing a resource that would otherwise be considered waste and need to be disposed of somewhere within our ecosystem. It is possible to obtain such waste oil in large quantities and often for free from restaurants that use deep fat friers. It will need to be filtered and processed to produce a useable fuel first but there are workshops available teaching the necessary skills to do this at home (see resources p185).

Biodiesel cannot be used in petrol engines. To run one you will need bioethanol.

BIOETHANOL

It is not just oils that can be utilised as biofuels. Other garden/agricultural waste also has the potential to be processed into fuel. Interestingly Henry Ford built his first engines to run on bioethanol. Bioethanol is alcohol produced from fermenting and distilling natural plant sugars or starches. It burns up to 85% cleaner than fossil fuels. Cellulosic ethanol can be made from old stalks, woodchips, grasses and other plant matter that would otherwise be composted at the time of harvesting. If you wanted to run a car entirely from this kind of fuel the engine would need to be modified first by, for example, changing the spark timings. However blending anything from 10-85% ethanol with regular petrol (gasoline) would not require modifications. Like biodiesel, bioethanol is a good solvent and so can degrade certain plastics and rubber that you would find in older cars. So if you don't carry out any modifications before using bioethanol, even in small amounts, you will need to remain alert for any signs of disintegrating tubes and seals.

Cellulosic ethanol requires a greater amount of processing than sugar rich ethanol which is most often used in commercial blends and is commonly made from sugar cane or corn. Making ethanol is apparently not too complex, although you will need to build a still first. If you are interested in producing your own ethanol at home with garden waste I suggest you read literature dedicated to the subject or attend a workshop.

It is very important to note that ethanol is for use in a petrol, not a diesel engine.

Biomethanol

This is created by gasification of organic materials. Regular methanol is the gasification of fossil fuels. It is less flammable than gasoline and can be put out with water as it breaks down in the presence of water. Like other biofuels it is harder to start in cold weather and so will need blending with petroleum but this is advisable anyway, otherwise its solvent action would break down seals within the engine. It is significantly more complex to produce than ethanol but still manageable on a small scale at home.

Biogas

Biogas is created from the fermentation of plant and/or animal waste to produce gases, methane being the most common one, forming 50-80% of the final product. The organic matter used can even be leaf litter or sewerage sludge. It is fermented in an anaerobic digester and then burned and used in a similar way to natural gas. It can be utilised in vehicle engines or used to generate electricity. A by-product of digesters is digestate. High in organic matter it can be incorporated into the soil where it will improve soil structure and add nutrients, acting as a natural soil fertiliser.

To conclude it is possible to produce significant quantities of biofuels on a small scale at home or as part of a co-operative. On a larger scale they need to be developed with a sustainable ethos in mind, without using conventional farming methods or encroaching on fertile crop land or ancient forest. If biofuels are to become a truly sustainable future option and a viable alternative to fossil fuels there is a need to change the way we use fuels and energy. Cleaner and more efficient technologies need to be developed alongside a reappraisal of what our needs really are and the adjustment of our behaviour and lifestyles in accordance.

A final piece of food for thought is 'myconol', produced when fungal sugars are mixed with yeast and other active ingredients. The result is a fuel, no different to ethanol, that can be combined with petrol (gasoline) to fuel cars. Still in its infancy the development of myconol, literally fuel from mushrooms, is being developed by eminent mycologist Paul Stamets and promises to be another great future alternative to fossil fuels, so watch this space!

NOTES

40. *"What is Biodiesel?"* www.biodiesel-fuel.co.uk.

CONCLUSION

A single plant can form an amazing resource base, providing the raw materials to meet a wide diversity of our needs. Growing a collection of different but equally resource rich plants combined with a good imagination and the inclination to experiment will make us much less vulnerable to commodity price rises resulting from a scarcity of resources. Using the finite resources we have wisely, appropriate use of technology and a change in consumption patterns will help smooth the transition to a more sustainable world. Growing exceptional plants, learning about their inherent resources and how to utilise them will enrich our lives. In so doing we become part of the process, our sense of connection to the natural world deepens and we feel more truly a part of it. The sense of value and level of respect for everything we use automatically becomes elevated in our consciousness, requiring us to act differently and to take full responsibility for our actions and their outcomes. These factors alone can change the world, filling it with respect and hope and allowing the post peak oil landscape to be one of abundance and satisfaction.

This is not a hippy utopia that is fluttering in my dreams, like 1000 butterflies disturbed from their salt lick all at once: I *know* this information and this angle of piecing the world together is a doorway to the truth. Taking responsibility for yourself is *all* you can do and voting through your actions and wallet are your truth and probably the most powerful choices you can make in this society. No amount of protesting or moaning will change a single thing unless we each start with an honest look at ourselves, our habits and most importantly our relationship with the world. It is our world and there is no separation - to think so is the greatest illusion of all. So deepen your knowledge, learn new skills and build up a resource base in your own backyard. These plants and others you will discover could unlock the change in yourself and the rest of human society we have all been waiting for, praying for and dreaming of.

APPENDIX I:
GUIDELINES FOR MAKING AND USING PLANT REMEDIES

WHENEVER I HARVEST a plant for any use I always ask the plant for permission first, explaining what I would like to use it for and thank it after. I find this approach especially important when you are using plants as medicines, in effect asking for their help. Approaching them respectfully as living beings will enhance the potency of the medicines you make and increase your connection to them.

If you are suffering an ongoing condition, are pregnant, breast feeding or are currently taking prescribed medication, consult with a health care professional before commencing the use of plant medicines to check for any drug interactions or cautions you should be aware of. Always start with a small amount of any plant medicine and increase it slowly. Be alert for any signs of allergy or undesirable side effects.

Each preparation mentioned within the plant directory is detailed here with recommended dosages. Do not exceed recommended dosages and double check with the relevant plant section as lower dosages may be appropriate where the plant gives especially strong medicine. If you are administering the remedies to minors give only one third of the recommended dosage to 3-11 year olds and half to 12-16 year olds.

It is essential to sterilize any bottles, jars and lids before storing remedies in them. Either put in the dishwasher on a hot wash, boil them in a large pan of water for 10 minutes or place in the oven and heat up to 160°C (320°F). When it reaches this temperature turn off the oven and let the jars cool before use.

PREPARATIONS AND DOSAGES

BATH

Place 30g fresh or 20g dried herb in a muslin bag under the taps as you run a bath and leave it bobbing in the water as you bathe. You will be absorbing the beneficial components through your skin and breathing the vapours in on the rising steam.

COMPRESS

To make a compress simply brew a strong infusion or decoction from the herb, soak a four-ply square of cloth or a flannel in it, wring some of the water out, then attach it to the affected area using a bandage or surgical tape. Compresses may be used hot or cold, although hot compresses should *never* be used when the skin is broken, for example with eczema, psoriasis or wounds. Leave on for a minimum of 30 minutes and a maximum of 8 hours, renewing as necessary. To keep a compress hot, hold a hot water bottle over it.

DECOCTION

Chop the roots or bark finely and leave in cold water over night and strain, then either drink cold or warm gently to your prefered drinking temperature. Alternatively, place the herb in cold water and heat until it begins to simmer. Allow it to simmer for 10-20 minutes before straining and drinking. Once strained it may be kept in the fridge for up to 2 days. Reheat the required amount before drinking. Use 1 teaspoon of dried or 2 teaspoons of fresh material per cup and drink a maximum of 3 cups daily unless stated otherwise in the text.

FLOWER ESSENCE

Make on a sunny morning when the flowers are newly opened. Fill a small glass bowl with spring water and cover the surface with freshly collected flowers. Leave the bowl on the ground in the sun for 3-4 hours then pour through a sieve or paper coffee filter to remove the flowers. Half fill a bottle with the flower water and top up with brandy to produce the 'mother' essence. This will stay good to use indefinitely. Further dilute this 'mother' essence before use by adding 7 drops to a 20ml dropper bottle filled with brandy. Use the essence from this second bottle, taking a couple of drops directly onto the tongue or adding it to a glass of water as needed. Take note of how you feel and how your emotions are affected and increase or lower the dosage as required. This is a very subtle yet suprisingly powerful way of using plant medicine.

FOOTBATH

Place a large handful of fresh plant matter (slightly less if using dried) in a washing up bowl, pour on boiling water then cover with a towel. Leave for 10 minutes to infuse and top up with cold water until it is at a comfortable temperature. Place your feet in the bowl, covering it back over with a towel to keep the vapours in. Soak your feet for at least 10 minutes.

GARGLE

Use a mouthful at a time of an infusion or decoction that has cooled to body temperature. Let your head fall back and the liquid swish around the back of your throat, making it bubble and gurgle by blowing air through it for approximately 45 seconds before spitting it out. This action may be repeated as needed.

INFUSED OIL

Always use a high quality organic oil as it will be absorbed through the skin into the body. It is preferable to use fresh plant matter but you can use dried if that is all you have available. Chop finely, place in a clean glass jar, thoroughly cover the plant matter with your choosen oil and seal with a screw cap. Leave for 3 weeks on a sunny window ledge, giving it a gentle shake every day. Line a sieve with muslin and pour the mixture through. Squeeze the remaining oil from the herbs and pour all of the oil into a dark glass container, labelling it clearly with the contents and date. Store away from bright light and use as needed by rubbing over the affected area. If you are making garlic oil for treating earache use olive oil for the base as it is naturally antibacterial and the prefered choice for use in the ear.

INFUSION

Make each cup by pouring boiling water over either 2 teaspoons of fresh herb or 1 teaspoon of dried, cover to prevent the volatile oils from escaping and leave to brew for 10 minutes. Strain before drinking. Drink 3 cups a day unless otherwise stated in the text.

JUICE

A good quality juicer is needed to extract juice from leaves (see resources p185 for suppliers). Recommended quantities for juicing are detailed in the text but where there are no recommended amounts simply consume the juice at your own discretion, ceasing use if you begin to suffer any adverse effects such as loose bowel movements.

MOUTHWASH

Take a mouthful of infusion or decoction that has cooled to body temperature and swill in the mouth for approximately 45 seconds before spitting out. Repeat as needed.

POULTICE

Mash the plant matter, moistening it with a little water if it is dry, to make a paste. Place the paste directly onto the affected area (or with a piece of cloth separating the skin and paste where direct contact with the skin is to be avoided) and hold the paste in place with a bandage. Leave it on for 30 minutes (or less if it causes irritation and longer if it feels fabulous).

SALVE

First make an infused oil then once 3 weeks have passed and the plant matter has been strained off, pour the oil into a pan and heat it very gently. Add 2g of beeswax for every 30ml of oil and stir while the wax melts. Drip the warm oil onto a plate where it will solidify quickly but will melt easily in response to the touch of a warm finger tip. If it is too firm add a little more oil to the pan and conversely if it is too soft add more wax. Once the consistency is correct pour into a dark glass screw cap jar, leave to solidify and thoroughly cool before adding the lid. If you put the lid on too soon it will be sucked on tightly as the salve cools and be very difficult to remove. Label clearly with the date and contents and store in a cool place away from direct light. Use as needed.

SLEEP PILLOW

Sew 2 pieces of fabric approximately 20 x 20cm together and fill with 100g of dried herbs. Place the pillow close to the head and inhale the slowly released herbal fragrances. The herbs should remain fragrant for at least 6 months but will fade gradually over time. Reuse the pillow by unstiching a corner, emptying and then refilling with a freshly dried batch of herbs.

SYRUP

Make a strong infusion/decoction using at least twice the usual quantity of herbs, then for every cup of liquid add the same volume of honey or sugar. Heat gently until all the honey/sugar has dissolved and the mixture has started to thicken. Pour into a glass container, label with the date and contents and store in the fridge where it should stay good for at least a year. Take 2 teaspoons 3 times daily as needed.

TINCTURE

Use finely chopped fresh plant matter if possible, place in a jar and cover with alcohol, making sure it is well covered and topping up the next day if necessary. Use either vodka or brandy that has a minimum strength of 40% vol. Leave to brew for 2 weeks, shaking vigourously once a day. Place a piece of muslin in a sieve and strain the mixture, squeezing the plant matter to extract the last concentrated bits of liquid. If you have a paper coffee filter pour it through this before bottling to remove any fine particles. Store in dark glass bottles, labeled with the date and contents. The tincture may last up to 5 or 6 years but it is preferable to make a new batch every year or two. Start with no more than 1ml (about a dropper full), building to a maximum of 3ml 3 times daily. Mix in a dash of water and drink but when administering to children mix in hot water so a little of the alcohol evaporates off.

Finally, for greater detail on how to work with medicinal plants and many more remedies using a much wider range of plants, get hold of a copy of my first book The Medicine Garden.

APPENDIX II:
COPPICE, FUEL WOOD AND CHARCOAL

DEMAND FOR WOOD has doubled in the UK since the 1950s, yet we can only provide for 12% of this demand with domestic supply. The danger when importing wood to meet this demand is that it may be tropical hardwood fresh from the rainforest. We all know the danger virgin forests and their inhabitants face worldwide, so the question is what are the sustainable alternatives? One is to only ever purchase FSC (Forest Stewardship Council) certified wood. The FSC are an independent, non-governmental, not-for-profit organisation that promotes the responsible management of the world's forests. If you see the FSC logo stamped on a piece of timber or a wood product you know there is a much better chance that it has been responsibly and sustainably sourced than if it does not display the logo. Another option, which is more of a personal and long term project, is to produce at least some of the wood you need yourself. The UK is dotted with coppice woodland that has gone out of production. These woodlands are often available and although not cheap, a group of friends with a few thousand pounds and a shared vision could easily acquire and restore a small coppice back into productivity. Equally, if you are blessed with owning a large acreage there are grant schemes in place which reward tree planting. The Royal Forestry Society produces a guide called 'Grants for Trees' which lists over 50 sources of funding available in the UK.

COPPICE

So what exactly is coppice? Well in short it is the cutting back of broad leaf trees to a stump or 'stool' just above ground level. This is done successionally and results in a number of straight branches growing to a roughly equal length and girth from the stump. Each tree species will take a different number of years to grow to a desirable size. Cropped in winter, new shoots are sent up from the stool the following spring and are left to grow for another full rotation of several years before harvesting again during the winter months. The stool remains intact and will remain productive for many, and in some cases hundreds of years if properly managed. In fact well managed coppicing can increase the lifespan of individual trees significantly. Some hazel stools found in eastern England are estimated to be over 1500 years old[41]. Coppicing also causes minimal soil disturbance and removes the need to constantly replace felled trees with saplings.

As the cycle completes and the 'underwood' (the poles that are cut from the stool) is harvested, light reaches the woodland floor and for a few years until the wood starts to thicken out again it provides a habitat where a more diverse range of plants will grow and insects thrive. If you are considering growing your own coppice or renovating a coppice that has fallen into neglect I would recommend attending a course where you can learn the skills necessary to generate a healthy and productive system (see resources p185).

A major compromise of coppicing is that the nut yield will be much lower than on a standard tree and it will only produce these nuts towards the end of its rotation. You could, however, simply leave some trees amongst your coppice to grow into standards to provide your nuts. The wood produced from a coppice can be put to many uses, one of which is fuel wood.

FUEL WOOD

I am currently typing this with 4 layers on my upper body, leggings, jeans, a scarf and fingerless gloves! It is reportedly the coldest winter for 30 years. This may be an anomaly but as the North Atlantic drift is set to slow or stop entirely as one of the predicted effects of climate change, these kinds of prolonged spells of subzero temperatures may well become more common. We have experienced great price hikes in gas and electricity over the last few years and gas, like oil, is a finite resource and so adds to our current predicament of fuel insecurity. These facts have driven many to uncover boarded up fireplaces, refurbish old chimneys, discard gas fires and replace them with modern efficient wood burners or use them as open fire places. It seems like a great idea. Wood is a renewable resource after all and weight for weight dry wood contains almost as much energy as coal. However, from what I have experienced demand is outstripping supply. Three years ago ½ a 'load' (approximately ½ a tonne) cost £60 in my area and now it costs £80; a 25% price increase in just 3 years and worse than that, by the end of the season as spring arrives it is increasingly difficult to get wood from any of my usual suppliers as they tend to run out during the winter months.

The solution? Effectively managed fast growing coppice and if you don't wanting to rely too heavily on others it might be a good idea to grow your own. It is suggested that a typical three bedroomed home would need around 3 hectares (7.5 acres) of mixed coppice in a ten year rotation to be fully self-sufficient in wood for heating. Of course size of house, level of insulation, type of wood and efficiency of the burner will all affect this figure. A well built and insulated home with a southern aspect (in the northern hemisphere) and a thermal mass wall would need very little if any fuel wood to maintain a comfortable temperature. However we all must make the most of what we have. As the majority of people simply do not have access to great acreages they can put down to coppice it may be heartening to know that as little as a quarter acre of short rotation willow coppice can be sufficient to meet the annual heating needs of a well insulated house with an efficient burner. I can almost guarantee in the current situation you would be able to sell on any surplus at what seems to be an ever increasing premium.

Freshly cut 'green' wood is very difficult to light, causes tar deposits in stoves and chimneys and burns at a much lower temperature, producing less heat than dry or 'seasoned' wood. It is best to burn wood that has a moisture content of no higher than 25% and it takes most species at least 6 months to reduce its moisture content to such a level, with some species taking much longer. Any firewood seasoned for 2 years will be sufficiently dry to burn well. Once the wood has been stored for 3 years woodworm, fungi and other biota will have gained a significant foothold and may be advanced in their purpose of breaking down and digesting the wood, making it a less efficient fuel. Wood does not conduct heat well so it proves

more efficient to burn smaller pieces than huge logs. The optimum size for woodburners, open fires and charcoal making is logs with a diameter of no more than 10cm. Split your logs and cut them to a size ready for burning soon after the wood has been harvested as this will expose more of the wood to the air, allowing it to season more rapidly. Newly cut wood should be stacked and will dry without covering over the summer but during the wetter months it is preferable to stack it in an open sided shelter and always as close to the point of use as possible. Wood in a closed shed is more likely to rot than dry properly as ventilation is essential if rotting is to be avoided. As the wood dries it loses weight, so if buying fuel wood by weight check whether it has been seasoned or not. In addition to using logs for fuel, wood is increasingly being converted to wood chips and burnt either in domestic wood chip boilers for heat and hot water production or in more industrial settings for both heat production and electricity generation.

Efficiency is affected by how and where you burn your wood. Open fires only have a 15-25% efficiency, free standing stoves have up to 70% while central heating wood chip boilers are the most efficient by far with an incredible 85-90% efficiency [42].

If you are concerned about the environmental implications of burning wood for warmth it is worth bearing in mind that no more carbon dioxide is released in burning wood than would be if the tree were left to rot and decompose in situ in the forest. If you season your wood well it will burn hot with very little smoke so your fire will not be adding small particulates into the atmosphere that form air pollution and are harmful when inhaled.

Of course in addition to obtaining firewood from coppice it can also be produced during thinning, felling, hedging, pruning and other operations, both in a suburban setting and commercially. I have a few trees on my boundaries that occasionally need cutting back and a few fruit trees which I prune. This provides a small proportion of my fuel wood needs. There is nothing quite as satisfying as chopping wood you have seen grow, plus of course you get the benefit of it heating you while wielding the axe on a winter's afternoon and then again as you carry it to or from your store and that is all before you even get it close to a flame.

I love it when I start my fire as it gives a moment of pause. I watch as the fire takes, learning which type and size of wood best encourages the flames to grow. I also take time at this point to thank the trees for the wood I have taken and the warmth they provide. Something magical happens around a fire. The warmth is not just physical, it creates an atmosphere of intimacy where people come together and share stories and laughter. Then finally collect the ash and recycle this by-product by sprinkling it over brassica and allium beds, soft fruits and fruit trees, the potash providing nutrients for your growing crops.

CHARCOAL

To produce charcoal wood needs to be burned slowly and this is done by restricting the supply of

oxygen. If the wood burns too quickly it will simply produce a pile of ash as it does on an open fire or a woodburner. To restrict the oxygen you will need a charcoal kiln with vents which can then control the levels of oxygen reaching the burning pile. Charcoal production requires a degree of expertise and regular access to your kiln whilst it's in use to ensure it is burning evenly. The end product is good quality charcoal that will light easily, negating the need for lighter fuel on your summer barbecue.

Home produced charcoal is a much more sustainable option than buying charcoal imported from the Far East where you will be unsure just how ethically it was produced and whether mature forests or mangroves were damaged or destroyed to provide you with coals for your summer indulgence. Charcoal produced from temperate woods is lighter than that produced from tropical hardwoods, is easier to light and reaches cooking temperatures (for barbecues) more quickly. Even if you are not in a position to produce your own charcoal it is worth trying to find producers in your local area who are managing coppice and selling charcoal as one of their products. Both the local community and local wildlife will benefit if you choose to support them.

Home produced charcoal will have a significantly higher commercial value than firewood, although the work involved may negate this price increase. There are commercial charcoal burners that travel from wood to wood and will produce charcoal for you. Alternatively the BTCV publication 'Woodlands: A

Practical Handbook' has in depth detail on how to do it with a ring kiln or a simple 45 gallon steel drum. Patrick Whitefield describes using a similar metal drum to make a mobile retort kiln in his book 'The Earth Care Manual'. A retort kiln is more efficient as it is a closed system, the burning wood remaining on the outside while the gases created during the process inside the kiln are released via a chimney. A ring kiln has the fire inside so some of the wood will be sacrificed in the process of making the charcoal. If you are interested in making your own why not go on a course (see resources p185) or look into the possibility of starting a charcoal makers' cooperative in your area where you can share equipment and skills with other similar minded folk.

NOTES

41. Piers Warren, *"British Native Trees: Their Past And Present Uses"* (Wildeye, 2006), 11.

42. *"Using Wood For Fuel"* Agroforestry News Volume 15, Number 2, February 2007, 15.

APPENDIX III:
INOCULATING LOGS WITH MUSHROOM SPAWN

SWEET CHESTNUT AND birch both play good hosts to mushroom spawn, especially shiitake and oyster mushrooms, and can be very productive. Take a log approximately 45cm long with a diameter of 10-15cm, drill holes 12cm apart around the log, fill with impregnated sawdust or plugs and seal with a dab of wax. Sawdust and plugs can be purchased from specialist suppliers (see resources p185). Plugs are more expensive but are

easier to use as the sawdust can easily dry out, killing the spawn before it gets a chance to colonise the log. Stack and store your logs in a shady and preferably damp place with one end slightly raised above the other. It will take up to two years for the mycelium to fully colonise sweet chestnut and usually a little less time for birch. Once you can see plenty of white mycelium strands covering both ends of the log you will need to shock them by immersing them in water for 48 hours. The mushrooms will suddenly burst into life with a crop usually being ready within a week. This process can be repeated up to four times a year. Logs will remain productive for 3-4 years, after which you can stick them in the woodburner or leave them to decompose, providing a mini habitat for wildlife.

RESOURCES

Most of the resources listed in this section are based in the UK and were current at the time of going to press, however, if you live elsewhere or find the businesses are no longer active then just do an internet search and you should find a supplier local to you.

PLANTS:

(to help you find some of the more unusual or specialist plants/ trees in the directory)

www.agroforestry.co.uk is a wonderful resource selling all kinds of interesting and unusual trees. They also run courses on forest gardening and publish a quarterly newsletter on temperate trees and shrub crops called Agroforestry News.

www.davids-exoticplants.co.uk (banana & monkey puzzle)

www.easytropicals.com (bamboo, banana, birch & monkey puzzle)

www.hardybananas.co.uk

www.hardyexotics.co.uk (bamboo & banana)

www.junglegiants.co.uk (bamboo)

www.mammothwillow.co.uk

www.mulu.co.uk (bamboo & banana)

www.thegarlicfarm.co.uk

www.thewillowbank.com (willow cuttings and living willow workshops)

INFORMATION

www.guerillagardening.org provides information and encouragement for any budding guerilla gardener.

The US based Institute for Local Self Reliance www.ilsr.org is a great resource with information covering everything from sustainable plastics to recycling with some useful links.

www.permaculture.co.uk produces a quarterly magazine called Permaculture. It is a great resource with interesting and inspiring articles. The permaculture association www. permaculture.org.uk lists courses and has some general information about permaculture. www.permacultureplanet.com is a great online resource with a global directory listing all kinds of permaculture groups, workshops, projects and jobs worldwide.

Ken Fern's wonderful book 'Plants For A Future' along with its associated website www.pfaf. org is an incredible resource listing over 7000 plants, so if you are looking for some more suggestions I would recommend this as a good place to start.

www.thelaststraw.org publishes The International Journal of Straw Bale and Natural Building, a quarterly magazine.

PRODUCTS

Food dehydrators and good quality juicers that can be used for juicing leaves can be sourced at www.ukjuicers.com or www.juiceland.co.uk.

Mushroom spawn can be purchased as either plugs or sawdust from www.annforfungi.co.uk, www.gourmetmushrooms.co.uk (also with training courses to help you get started), and www.fungi.com (USA) or www.mushroompatch.com (USA and Canada only).

Sprout bags can be purchased at www.juiceland.co.uk.

www.oilseedpress.co.uk supplies both small kitchen counter seed presses and larger, more industrial equipment for cold pressing nuts and seed. They can be contracted to press larger amounts and will bottle the oil for you. Nuts can also be cold pressed at home with a millstone if you have one! www.agoilpress.com is a US company producing precision cold screw presses which are useful for larger amounts and has links to suppliers in the US and Canada.

CRAFTS & COURSES

www.cat.org.uk offers a wealth of courses including woodland management, charcoal making, willow sculpture, green wood crafts and much more.

www.cleftwood.co.uk run by Richard de Trey-White in Wiltshire offers individual and group tuition in cleftwood chair/furniture making and pole lathe turning.

www.durston.org.uk is a smallholding that runs workshops on making biodiesel from waste vegetable oil.

www.fransbrown.co.uk offers tuition in wood turning and sells Frans Browns's beautiful handcrafted pieces.

I teach how to make salves, oils, tinctures and other plant remedies. For up to date course information visit www.gatewaystoeden.com.

www.guidooakleydesign.com provides useful items for the garden, home and office by master craftsman and sculptor Guido Oakley.

www.norahkennedywillowworker.co.uk is based in Gloucestershire and produces willow baskets and sculptures. Norah Kennedy runs workshops teaching willow weaving to make baskets and other structures.

www.wildwoodcrafts.com is run by Dave Jackson in Worcestershire and teaches coppice crafts including coppice restoration, hedge laying and making rustic furniture and living wood structures.

GLOSSARY

ALA – alpha linolenic acid.

ADHD – attention deficit hyperactivity disorder.

ARTERIOSCLEROSIS – the build up of fatty deposits on the artery walls which, over time, causes hardening and narrowing of the arteries combined with a loss of elasticity. In its advanced state it increases the risk of suffering from blood clots, stroke, heart failure, kidney failure and high blood pressure.

ASTRINGENT – a substance which causes the contraction of tissues and the drying up of secretions and bleeding.

BACH FLOWER REMEDIES – originally developed by Dr Edward Bach an English physician in the 1930s to treat people's underlying emotional conditions.

CITES - the Convention on International Trade in Endangered Spieces of Wild Fauna and Flora.

CLEFT – wood that has been split along the grain as opposed to sawn. This process will leave the wood stronger as the grain remains intact.

EFA – essential fatty acid. Our bodies cannot make them and yet requires them for efficient functioning, so they must be obtained from external sources such as food.

FAGGOT – a bundle of sticks. It was once a measuring unit but now it can really refer to any bundle of sticks regardless of the proportion.

GLA – gamma-linoleic acid.

HDL – high density lipoproteins (or 'good' cholesterol).

HURDLE – temporary fence or screen.

IBS – irritable bowel syndrome.

LDL – Low density lipoproteins (or 'bad' cholesterol).

MDF – medium density fibreboard. Used in all kinds of interior furnishings it is a composite material made from waste wood fibres glued together with resin, pressure and heat. The resin contains formaldehyde which will leak from the board during construction and after if it is not properly sealed.

NERVINE – a nerve tonic which acts therapeutically on the nerves, often as a sedative, quieting nervous excitement and calming anxiety.

PMS – premenstrual syndrome.

SVO – straight vegetable oil.

THC - tetrahydrocannabinol.

BIBLIOGRAPHY

Agate, Elizabeth *Woodlands: A Practical Handbook* BTCV Publications, 1980

Andrews, George & Vikenoog, Simon(editors) *The Book Of Grass: An Anthology On Indian Hemp* Peter Owen Ltd., 1967

Bacon, Gretchen (editor) *Celebrating Birch: The Lore, Art and Craft of an Ancient Tree* Fox Chapel Publishing Company Inc., 2007

Baines, Patricia *Flax and Linen* Shire Publications Ltd., 1985

Bell, Michael *The Gardener's Guide To Growing Temperate Bamboos* David & Charles Publishers, 2000

Borseth, Kolbjørn *The Aromantic Guide to Unlocking the Powerful Health & Rejuvenation Benefits of Vegetable Oils* Aromantic Ltd., 2008

Brown, Deni *The Royal Horticultural Society Encyclopedia of Herbs & Their Uses* Dorling Kindersley, 1995

Bunn, Stephanie *Working With Living Willow* Woodland Craft Supplies, 1999

Conway, Peter *Tree Medicine: A Comprehensive Guide to the Healing Power of Over 170 Trees* Judy Piatkus Ltd., 2001

Corby, Rachel *The Medicine Garden* The Good Life Press Ltd., 2009

Cornett, James W *How Indians Used Desert Plants* Nature Trails Press, 2002

Cunningham, Scott *Encyclopaedia of Magical Herbs* Llewellyn Publications, 1985

Evert Hopman, Ellen *Tree Medicine, Tree Magic* Phoenix Publishing Inc., 1991

Fern, Ken *Plants for a Future; Edible & Useful Plants for a Healthier World* Permanent Publications, 1997

Flowerdew, Bob *Bob Flowerdew's Organic Bible: Successful Gardening the Natural Way* Kyle Cathie Ltd., 1998

Joiner-Bey, Herb *The Healing Power of Flax* Freedom Press, 2004

Kato, Yoshio *Garlic: The Unknown Miracle Worker* Oyama Garlic Laboratory, 1973

Lavelle, Christine & Michael *The Organic Garden: A Practical Guide to Natural Gardens, from Planning and Planting to Harvest and Maintenance* Anness Publishing, 2003

Law, Ben *The Woodland Year* Permanent Publications, 2008

McCabe, John *Sunfood Living: Resource Guide for Global Health* Sunfood Publishing, 2007

Meyerowitz, Steve *Kitchen Garden Cookbook* Sproutman Publications, 1983

Meyerowitz, Steve *Sprouts the Miracle Food: The Complete Guide to Sprouting* Sproutman Publications, 1983

Mobbs, Paul *Energy Beyond Oil* Matador Publishing, 2005

Mollison, Bill & Holmgren, David *Permaculture One* First published by Transworld Publishers (Australia) Pty. Ltd., 1978. This edition; Tagari Publications, 1990

Neal's Yard Remedies *Make Your Own Cosmetics* Haldane Mason, 1997

Robinson, Rowan *The Hemp Manifesto: 101 Ways That Hemp Can Save Our World* Park Street Press, 1997

Roulac, John W *Hemp Horizons: The Comeback of the World's Most Promising Plant* Chelsea Green Publishing Company, 1997

Sanderson, Liz *How To Make Your Own Herbal Cosmetics: The Natural Way To Beauty* Latimer New Dimensions Ltd., 1977

Stangler, Carol *The Craft & Art of Bamboo* Lark Books, 2001

Stuart, Malcolm (editor) *The Encyclopedia of Herbs and Herbalism* MacDonald & Co. Ltd., 1979

Warren, Piers *British Native Trees: Their Past and Present Uses* Wildeye, 2006

Warren, Piers *101 Uses for Stinging Nettles* Wildeye, 2006

Whitefield, Patrick *The Earth Care Manual* Permanent Publications, 2004

Whitefield, Patrick *Woodland in Permaculture* Patrick Whitefield, 1992

Wigmore, Ann *The Wheatgrass Book* Avery, 1985

WEBSITES

www.bbccountryfilemagazine.com/feature/real-food/truth-about-spelt

www.biodiesel-fuel.co.uk

www.glasu.org.uk/en/uploads/documents/WelshThatchingStraw.pdf

www.globaltrees.org/tp_monkeypuzzle.htm

http://www.promusa.org/component/content/article/160-scientists-produce-fuel-using-parts-of-the-banana-plant

www.sciencedaily.com (Queen's University, Belfast (2009, October 9) Banana Plants May Be Used In Production Of Plastic Products.)

www.wisegeek.com/what-is-a-temperate-zone.htm

JOURNALS AND OTHER PUBLICATIONS

Agroforestry News, Volume 13, Number 3, May 2005.

Agroforestry News, Volume 15, Number 2, February 2007.

Agroforestry Research Trust, Factsheet S07, Edible Tree Saps

Green Earth News, 30 August 2009, *Bamboo is Destroying our Planet* by Doug Bancorn

Permaculture, No.65, Autumn 2010, *Thinking Globally Acting Locally* by Patrick Whitefield

The Malawi Nation, 12 November 2005, *Hunger Takes Toll in Salima* by George Ntonya

"Clearly we could not live without the plants and trees, so this is my ode to them, my song of appreciation and my invitation for you to not only see them as a wonderful and immense array of living and constantly growing and renewing resources but as companions, as other living beings with whom we share this life and upon whom we depend. I invite you to acknowledge, love and respect them and with them shape your environment, the patch of earth that you are stewarding in this life time, to one where we can all thrive and live abundant and joyful lives gaining pleasure and sustenance from each other".

Rachel Corby

About the Author

Rachel Corby is a gardener and a medicine woman. She has spent many years on environmental projects around the globe, learning about plants in their natural setting and how they can be used to heal degraded landscapes. This led to her studying both permaculture and sustainable land use with Patrick Whitefield. She subsequently worked in a herb nursery for several years, where she began to learn the therapeutic benefits of plants relating to human health.

The quest to deepen her relationship with plants took her to local medicinal herbalists and medicine men as far and wide as the Amazon basin to the Highlands of Kenya, where she discovered the healing qualities of plants on not only the physical, but also the emotional and spiritual levels. This has culminated in a working knowledge of folk medicine.

She has completed a 9 month apprenticeship in Sacred Plant Medicine with Stephen Harrod Buhner and, combining this with her previous training in Plant Spirit Medicine, she now teaches, passing on these beautiful and ancient ways of working with plants. She believes that learning to communicate with plants and nature helps bring a powerful sense of balance and healing, not only for the individual but also the wider environment.

For information and workshop dates please visit
www.gatewaystoeden.com

The Good Life Press Ltd.
The Old Pigsties, Clifton Fields
Lytham Road, Preston
PR4 0XG
01772 633444

The Good Life Press is a family run business publishing a wide range of titles for the smallholder, 'goodlifer' and farmer. We also publish **Home Farmer,** the monthly magazine for anyone who wants to grab a slice of the good life - whether they live in the country or the city. Other titles of interest: